Role of Government in a Market Economy

Role of Government in a Market Economy

EDITED BY

LOWELL D. HILL

Iowa State University Press
AMES, IOWA

© 1982 The Iowa State University Press. All rights reserved

Composed and printed by The Iowa State University Press, Ames, Iowa   50010

First edition, 1982

Library of Congress Cataloging in Publication Data
Main entry under title:

Role of government in a market economy.

    1. Agriculture and state—United States—Addresses, essays, lectures. 2. Agricultural price supports—United States—Addresses, essays, lectures. 3. Agriculture—Economic aspects—United States—Addresses, essays, lectures. 4. United States—Economic policy—1981——Addresses, essays, lectures. I. Hill, Lowell D.
HD1761.R64   1982   338.1′873   82-17298
ISBN 0-8138-1576-2

C O N T E N T S

v

Laurence J. Norton, 1896–1956

P R E F A C E

THE NORTON LECTURE SERIES was made possible by an endowment established by Aurene T. Norton in memory of Laurence J. Norton. Laurence J. Norton—teacher, author, counselor, and research director—made numerous contributions in several areas related to agricultural economics. His interest lay primarily in the area of agricultural policy and marketing. His belief in the importance of a free market was strong and consistent throughout his professional career: "I admit a bias toward free markets as a mechanism for getting foods produced and distributed. My considered opinion is that in providing adequate food for basic human needs, a free market will operate more effectively than any program involving planned marketing, price controls, state trading, or any of the devices which planners can conceive in efforts to plan production, distribution, and consumption." It is quite appropriate that the first lecture series dedicated to the memory of Dr. Norton should focus on the role of government in agricultural markets.

The chapters in this book were drawn from lectures delivered at the University of Illinois, Urbana, and from the discussions stimulated by the lecturers. Each examines the issue from a different perspective. Chapter 1 provides a historical review of the definition of markets and the functions that markets perform. It identifies some of the structural changes that have taken place in agricultural markets, their causes, and the direction of future changes. Chapter 2 identifies an approach for evaluating the performance of market systems with different degrees of government involvement in marketing. Chapter 3 examines the economic environment in which agricultural markets operate—the fiscal and monetary policies and changing work ethic in the United States that limit the ability of the market to respond to supply and demand. Chapter 4 identifies the distortions of the market caused by market power of large firms and suggests alternatives in antitrust policies that can keep the market system operating. Chapter 5 describes the strengths and weaknesses of the market and separates the objectives of society that can be met best by a free market from those that must be left to government agencies. Chapter 6 looks at U.S. exports and world trade and how they have been influenced by government actions. One action by government (for example, the suspension of grain sales to the Union of Soviet Socialist Republics) inevitably leads to the need for other actions to provide protection for firms disadvantaged by the first action. The cumulative effects of an increased government role in price, income, and trade policies have influenced the comparative advantage of U.S. agriculture and the structure of world trade. Chapter 7 looks more specifically at agricultural policies in the 1980s and their relationships with the macroeconomics of the Reagan administration.

The seven chapters have been prepared over a period of three years in a rapidly changing domestic and world economic environment. Some of these situational differences are reflected in the illustrations used by the different authors. However, the validity of the principles and concepts in the chapters is independent of the time period in which each was written.

The lecture by H. F. Breimyer was presented as a departmental seminar on November 29, 1977. J. K. Galbraith presented the first public lecture in October 1979. Three public lectures were given during 1980—W. F. Mueller, April 17; T. W. Schultz, June 11; and D. G. Johnson, September 25. The final lecture in the series was presented November 30, 1981, by B. L. Gardner.

There is considerable diversity of opinion among the authors as to the causes and solutions of agricultural problems. Lecturers were intentionally selected to emphasize the differences. The book provides no consensus on the proper role of government in agricultural markets, but it should help the readers order and evaluate their own beliefs about this important issue.

LOWELL D. HILL

Role of Government in a Market Economy

1

Markets and Prices
in Today's Agricultural Economy

HAROLD F. BREIMYER

PERHAPS strangely, the terms "markets" and "prices" are so ingrained in the language of agricultural economists that few have written about them as abstract concepts. The following two citations illustrate two different ways of conceptualizing an economy structurally organized around the institutions of markets and prices. Warren Samuels expresses what he regards as Charles Edwin Ayres's notion of orthodox economics. He thinks it represents "a secularized cultural tradition of natural order philosophy. . . . Economic theory is *price* theory because 'price has been conceived as the locus of a system of reciprocal forces which automatically regulates the economic order. . . .' "[1]

An entirely different characterization comes from the French economist Gerard Debreu, who refers to "the explanation of the price of commodities resulting from the interaction of the agents of a private ownership economy."[2]

I prefer the second of these quotations because Debreu sees price as resulting from the interaction of human agents. That, in my judgment, is distinctly the most felicitous way of expressing how a market economy operates. Supply and demand are only abstract concepts of forces at work that help to account for human behavior. Economic activity is carried on by human beings.

My final introductory note draws on a Boulding quotation. In the kind of cryptic language for which that creative gentleman is well

Harold F. Breimyer is Perry Foundation Professor of Agricultural Economics, University of Missouri, Columbia.

known, Boulding declares that "the ultimate value for which all tools are used and which all instrumental values serve is ceremony."[3]

The meaning of this adage will be obscure to some and scarcely acceptable to others, as it alleges that performance patterns in economics can become elevated to symbolism. Virtually sanctified, they are accepted as verities no longer subject to inquiry or challenge. This can be an unpropitious development and truly opposite to (and the enemy of) scientific investigation. I will return to this point later.

It is time to attempt my own coinage as to what is meant by a system of markets and prices in which price is not only the ratio in market exchange but an effectuating instrument. It seems that price, though an exchange ratio, represents the culmination of negotiation between sovereign entities, definitely not performed under duress, resulting in transfer of entitlement to a good or service. According to this definition there must be fulfillment and completion, the approximate equivalent of the lawyer's idea of consideration in a contract. It describes a working, functional relationship.

Clearly, this concept involves much more than the posting of an offer to sell or a bid to buy. In no sense is it a transfer price within an entity or a bookkeeping entry.

MARKETS AND PRICES IN EVOLUTIONARY DEVELOPMENT

Probably every economist of my cohort joins in regretting the little attention now accorded economic history in graduate curricula. The record of the evolutionary emergence of markets and prices as institutions carries a great deal of meaning. Nearly everyone knows that market transactions revolving around price grew out of the Middle Ages and that they were a dramatic development, a sharp contrast to the conventional economic system they supplanted. Polanyi is one of the most eloquent chroniclers. He emphasizes the idea that there had to be an economic order separate from the social order before our kind of economy could take form.[4] That separation was unprecedented. Thurnwald expresses the same idea by saying that the whole fabric of feudal society had to be transformed before a market system could emerge.[5]

We of our generation who take a market exchange system as a given fail to appreciate that its striking feature is not the instrument of price as such, though that is a necessary condition, but the sovereignty of each trader. Each party to a market transaction is an independent entity, possessing sovereignty and capable of truly discretionary action. Furthermore, for a system of markets to fulfill the welfare criteria that most of us apply, it must exhibit equivalence, that is, equity. Bargaining power is not an imaginary idea. The comfortable assumption that exchange divides benefits about equally, regardless of relative bargaining position, simply is not valid as a generalized proposition. This issue has attracted most attention in recent years in the context of trade among nations. The textbook axiom was that trade between two nations benefits both parties, even with the inference that the two benefit about equally. McPherson is perhaps best known among agricultural economists who deny that felicitous outcome. He says that rich nation–poor nation trade can be exploitive (of the latter by the former).[6]

As a final word on the principle of sovereignty, the term "implicity" connotes entrepreneurial independence. A subunit in a vertically integrated organization does not have sovereignty. Within large firms there are many intertransfers using transfer or shadow prices, but those are not true prices in the sense of a market system. This point apparently is recognized and accepted.

My next observation may not meet so nearly universal approval. If markets and prices are genuinely to regulate an economy, price must dominate all other elements in transactions. In the U.S. economy of our era, price has progressively been subordinated. It has been subordinated to the many forms of nonprice competition. The fact that it has seldom been totally eliminated does not justify defensive arguments such as "Look, price is still here!" The relative role of price in transactions is a highly significant datum. As most persons know, price tends to have an almost uncontested role at the raw material level, including the trading of basic farm products. It is compromised more at later stages in the marketing sequence. One study indicates that consumers generally place price only fourth among the important considerations in their purchasing habits and the attractions of the vendor. Quality and variety of offerings come higher.[7]

It is a contradiction, and clearly asymmetrical, that whereas on the one hand the price of farm products is highly significant to the farmers who sell them, on the other hand it is of secondary importance and may be almost inconsequential to the processors who buy them. Various processors are much less concerned with the level of price than with uniformity of price to all buyers. My students are usually sur-

prised when I assign a reading by Knutson relative to pricing in milk
marketing. According to him, distributors are quick to say that the
overriding concern of each one regarding price is that he pay no more
than his competitors do.[8]

In the marketing of farm products from the farm, long supposed
to be the safest haven of price transactions, price as an active instrument (that is, as controlling spot transfer to title) in reality is on a pro-
gressive decline. A great deal of formula pricing has arisen, for example, as in eggs and dressed beef. It is usually based on a privately
reported supply-and-demand price. There is some committee pricing,
as in cotton. Fluid milk has distinctive price making. On the West
Coast particularly, but also in some milksheds, price bargaining is fairly common.

It is a temptation to carry this argument forward into the various
institutions of price discovery.[9] My principal and final message on this
subject is to testify to its importance. It belongs on every marketing
economist's agenda, to use Don Paarlberg's favorite term. Extension
economists have shown more alertness and originality in treating the
subject than either research or teaching economists.[10]

NECESSARY CONDITIONS FOR A SYSTEM OF MARKETS AND PRICES

Thus far my comments have been fairly conventional and not
often greatly disputed. The remarks that follow are not accepted as
conventional wisdom. They are more exploratory in nature.

As previously stated, markets and prices for farm products and
food came into general acceptance late in the Middle Ages. They
served almost exclusively to distribute product. Used in that way, commodity price is highly functional. Price will distribute; it will ration.
Perhaps its most idealized applicability is to a market-clearing operation. My colleague James Rhodes often emphasizes that the idealized
price-powered market is of the market-clearing variety.

Market clearing is far from the prevailing application of price
nowadays. Much of the price system utilizes administered price. As
Scitovsky insists, administered price is always an instrument of
power.[11] Its use may nor may not violate welfare criteria, but the
power concept is intrinsic. In this regard, farmers who sell into market-
clearing operations such as livestock auctions are painfully aware that
they lack the power that would let them administer the price. It even

seems that the call for a farmers' strike that has been heard from time to time can be interpreted as a desire to shift to administered pricing for farm products (in a search for favorable terms to farmers, of course) without accepting the discipline that necessarily accompanies administered pricing.

But if price works best and most easily in distributing products, the truly revolutionary application of price in the last few centuries has been the employment of price to allocate the factors of production that generate income and determine its distribution. Extension of price to these multiple roles was heroic indeed. To ask a single instrument to accomplish all three ends is to ask a lot. It follows that it is totally unjustified to assume in a kind of intellectual indolence that the rather ready acceptability of the efficiency of price in performing the first function automatically carries forward to the factor-allocation and income-distribution functions.

In reflecting on the three missions of price, I have formulated the following propositions that set forth the conditions that must prevail if exclusive reliance is to be placed on market exchange powered by price. These are as follows:

1. Sovereignty of the economic unit. The specifications of sovereignty and their violations amount to one way of describing the various models of imperfect competition. For example, a firm in oligopoly is not truly sovereign or at best can be regarded as having only conditional sovereignty. The reason is that rival firms can always counteract, to a degree, the steps a given firm may take.

2. Relatively easy access to physical resources. Basic resources such as land, water, ports, transport routes, metals, fossil fuels, and others are essential and must be available on nondiscriminatory terms, according to this thesis. For the moment, it is not necessary to distinguish between depletable and nondepletable resources nor to define "nondiscriminatory."

3. Industrial production techniques as the ultimate equalizer of income distribution. This is not the usual tribute to those techniques. One great merit of industrial techniques is that they are essentially egalitarian. This principle arises from the fundamental economics of constant returns to scale. When the plant is utilized fully, output-input ratios are technical in the long run.

For the sake of brevity I will not develop the idea of sovereignty.

This is usually treated in the context of industrial organization. Willard F. Mueller at the University of Wisconsin is the foremost exponent of this concept in agricultural economics.

With respect to item 2, in my judgment it is not an accident that presently received neoclassical economic theory evolved at a stage in history when the whole western world was expanding into continents of new resources and miracles of industrial technology were being invented and applied. These factors have obviously interacted gloriously, the ultimate instance of symbiosis.

It may seem strange today, when some Illinois farmland sells for $4,000 an acre, that until about two generations ago land was available almost for the taking. Furthermore, even as the new lands of the West were opened up and settled, they did not generate high values and rents to the older lands of the East. The situation contradicted the thesis of Ricardo, who said that as new marginal lands had to be opened up, the older lands would generate the unearned income known as rent. But our new lands of the West were better, not poorer, than those of the East.

As for minerals, including fossil fuels, until recently they were not only plentiful but made available at the cost of reaching them. Furthermore, we assumed for a long time that new discoveries would be equally as rich and accessible as the old.[12]

The theme that permeates all of the above discussion about highly accessible raw materials (and land) and achieving constant returns to scale in industrial production underpins the egalitarian (equitable distribution) aspects of marginal cost pricing. Manifestly, marginality is the sacred concept of neoclassical economists. When the circumstances described above prevail, marginal cost pricing genuinely attaches a product price consistent with the price of constituent factors of production and minimizes unearned income (rent). This is, in my judgment, an extremely fundamental observation with respect to what is known in economic theory as "the economics of welfare."

It follows that the more those conditions are violated, that is, the steeper the slope in the cost curve (aggregate), the greater is the proportion of rent returns. Rent, as is well known, is an unearned income and violative of our American creed in terms of rewarding contribution to production. Also, as history abundantly verifies, excessive rent shares in an economy can become socially disruptive.

As a quick digression, if rent exceeds what is socially acceptable, the two policy courses open are to tax it away or apply price discrimination to the products produced.

The conclusion follows that the steeper the slope of the cost curve, the more socially unacceptable is market pricing as the controlling force over income distribution.

PRICING OF DEPLETABLE RESOURCES

As an attempt to open relevant issues rather than close them with dogmatic conclusions, I offer brief observations leading to a strong plea for agricultural economists to give more attention henceforth to the economics of utilization of depletable raw material resources.

Manifestly, we are seeing more and more instances of sharply rising cost curves in operations that make various fossil fuels available and in metals also. For example, without exaggeration the delivery cost of petroleum in the United States ranges from about $1 per barrel in the older but still productive wells to the maximum price now received, about $34 per barrel. The curve keeps rising (potentially) until it reaches the stage at which the BTUs required to extract and deliver the oil equal the BTU content of the oil itself.

The same principles apply in some degree to farmland. No productive farmland lies unoccupied. Increased production comes at increased cost. A few inferences can be suggested.

The first relates to a pricing policy for energy. Marginal cost pricing will yield astronomical unearned income to older productive wells. Such an outcome violates all the welfare considerations we have associated with the economics of a market and price system. Why do so many economists refuse to admit the discrepancy? I suppose the answer is, to quote Professor Boulding once again, that we like to ceremonialize our economic propositions rather than to expose them to scrutiny.

A second point is that as basic resources become scarcer and more tightly held, Keynesian-type fiscal stimulation in the economy adds little to productivity but adds a great deal to the asset value of existing resources. The price of antique furniture can be used as a kind of index. One wonders which price has gone up most, that of Illinois soybean land or 1870 Seth Thomas clocks.

Third, rising asset value of farmland makes landholding much more attractive than land operating. This too I cannot develop here. It is appropriate for inquiry by a graduate student writing a master's thesis or Ph.D. dissertation.[13]

My final point is the one I promised. It is that we simply must give more attention to the economics of utilization and nonutilization (withholding) of mineral resources. As an oversimplified statement, the hypothesis I reach is that once it becomes recognized that resources can be depleted, the economics of extraction is no longer the economics of access, but is the economics of the depletion rate relative to anticipated future value, all interacting with the interest rate and liquidity pressure. That is to say, I find attractive the idea that depletable resources such as petroleum take on a temporal reservation price. The reservation price at any time is affected by forecasts as to how rapidly the price will increase in the future compared with the interest rate. If the price is expected to increase faster than the current interest rate, the incentive is to withhold. This is the rational decision except insofar as a firm may be under liquidity pressure.

Unfortunately, during the era in history when resources seemed limitless, little was written about the principles of the economics of depletion. In my own search I have been impressed by a few older articles that anticipated our time. One is by the famed land economist L. C. Gray.[14] A second, written in 1931, is by the imaginative general economist Harold Hotelling.[15] Then, at the 1977 meeting of the American Association of Agricultural Economists, Maurice Kelso gave as his Fellows lecture a stimulating inquiry into the same subject.[16] In eloquent language Kelso called on agricultural economists to enfold the economics of utilization of depletable resources into their investigations and expertise.

CONCLUSIONS

The idea that an economy can be self-regulating on the basis of markets and price is a heroic idea. It was almost fulfilled at one stage in the industrialization of Western economies. In my judgment it could reach fruition only if the ownership structure assured sovereignty of all units, if basic resources were readily available at a virtually uniform cost of access, and if industrial techniques were widely diffused and applied. In my observation, price is on a steady decline as an instrument in guiding our U.S. economy. It is even on a decline in agriculture, and in that connection I mention the gradual demise of open exchange markets in which product changes hands according to spot negotiation of price. I call attention to the extension study relating to marketing alternatives mentioned previously.

Because the second condition of ready availability of basic resources (minerals and land) is increasingly violated, I confess my apprehensions that the role of price will be compromised more and more in all parts of the economy that are sensitive to the terms of access to those resources. Agriculture is one of them. The economics of land is due for resurgence. However, equally important is the economics of the depletable resources that have provided the wherewithal for so many of the technological practices adopted in recent decades. Even though indulgence in the familiar call for more research is properly disparaged, my concluding note is indeed a petition that agricultural economists give more attention to the economics of raw materials. Professor Kelso's admonition is mine also.

NOTES

1. Warren J. Samuels, "The Knight-Ayres Correspondence: The Grounds of Knowledge and Social Action," *Journal of Economic Issues* (Sept. 1977): 487. The inserted quotation is from Charles Edwin Ayres, "Moral Confusion in Economics," *Ethics* (Jan. 1935):180.
2. Gerard Debreu, *Theory of Value, an Axiomatic Analysis of Economic Equilibrium,* Monograph 17 (New York: Cowles Foundation, 1959). Taken from Nicholas Kaldor, "The Irrelevance of Equilibrium Economics," *Economic Journal* (Dec. 1972):1237.
3. Kenneth E. Boulding, "A Review Symposium," *Journal of Economic Issues* (Sept. 1977):658.
4. Karl Polanyi, *The Great Transformation* (New York: Rinehart, 1944).
5. Richard Thurnwald, *Economics in Primitive Communities* (London Oxford University Press, 1932).
6. W. W. McPherson, "Role of Agricultural Trade in Economic Development," *Journal of Farm Economics* (May 1966):354–65.
7. Gosta Mickwitz, "The Means of Competition at Various Stages of Production and Distribution," *Kyklos* (Nov. 1958):509–20.
8. Ronald D. Knutson, "Buyer Strategy in Bilateral Oligopoly," *American Journal of Agricultural Economics* (Dec. 1968):1507–11.
9. A classification scheme for systems of price discovery is found in H. F. Breimyer, *Economics of the Product Markets of Agriculture* (Ames: Iowa State University Press, 1976), pp. 114–19.
10. Olan D. Forker and V. James Rhodes, eds., *Marketing Alternatives for Agriculture: Is There a Better Way?* Cornell University extension leaflets 7-1 to 7-13, Ithaca, N.Y., February 1976.
11. Tibor Scitovsky, *Welfare and Competition* (Homewood: Irwin, 1971), pp. 24–25.
12. Ibid., pp. 140–42.
13. Theoretical concepts that underlie much of this can be found in H. F. Breimyer, "The Three Economies of Agriculture," *American Journal of Agricultural Economics* (Aug. 1962):679–99; and "Agriculture's Three Economies in a Changing Environment," *American Journal of*

Agricultural Economics (Feb. 1978):37–47. The latter especially takes up
the matter of patterns of returns—increasing, decreasing, or constant—
and refers to now classic articles on the subject once familiar as "Empty
Economic Boxes."
14. Lewis C. Gray, "Rent under the Assumption of Exhaustibility,"
Quarterly Journal of Economics (May 1914):466–89.
15. Harold Hotelling, "The Economics of Exhaustible Resources," *Journal
of Political Economy* (Apr. 1931):137–75.
16. Maurice M. Kelso, "Natural Resource Economics: The Upsetting
Discipline," *American Journal of Agricultural Economics* (Dec. 1977):
814–23.

2

Evaluating the Performance of Agricultural Markets

LOWELL D. HILL

THE FREE-MARKET CONCEPT FOR AGRICULTURE

FREE MARKETS and competitive industries have been basic tenets in the idealized version of the U.S. economic system since the colonization of America. The free-market concept has continued as an ideal against which many economists, as well as the general public, judge economic performance. This performance norm is implicit in much of the anti-trust philosophy, in the objectives of farm programs debated in agricultural committees of Congress, and in the policy resolutions developed by many national farm organizations. The free-market, competitive-industry ideal has persisted despite the fact that no U.S. market is truly free or truly competitive. The trend since the industrial revolution, if not before, has been to substitute administrative controls for free-market forces. The substitution has been accomplished through changing market structure; direct government involvement in the marketplace; and public policies directly and indirectly concentrating market power in the hands of fewer and fewer individuals, corporations, and government agencies.

Agriculture and the service industries have often been identified as the last remaining examples of the competitive system operating in a free market. Although there are some vestiges of competition remaining in the farm sector (for example, large numbers of small farms), the significant role of government in the agricultural sector is

Lowell D. Hill is L. J. Norton Professor of Agricultural Marketing at the University of Illinois, Urbana.

not consistent with the structural attributes of a competitive industry. An industry in which 50 percent of production is concentrated on 4 percent of the farms and in which government payments have accounted for as much as 25 percent of net farm income clearly does not meet the basic test of competitive structure and free markets.

A free market, in the pure sense, can be defined as a system of exchange that is free from all government interference, regulation, or influence. Those who uphold agriculture as the example of pure competition in a free market and call for policies to return agriculture to a free-market industry are obviously not using this definition. The pure definition of a free market would exclude government enforcement of contracts, public collection of market information, and establishment of currency values. A market fitting such a definition of "free" would, if it existed, have little or no economic value. It would certainly not meet the needs of modern U.S. agriculture. Most proponents of "free markets for agriculture," if pressed, would reject the pure definition that excludes all government involvement in agriculture.

Having established that the pure definition of a free market is not what is intended by most people using the term, it is necessary to formulate a more workable definition. We can define a free market as a system of exchange in which prices are free to respond to the stimuli of demand and supply operating within a given economic and political environment. Prices are therefore set primarily by demand and supply forces, even though these forces may be influenced by public bodies and government actions.

Definitions can sometimes be clarified by describing contrasting alternatives. The antithesis of a free market is a market in which prices are established by government actions. The presence of government-determined prices is readily identified. The absence of such prices is less readily observed because nearly every action of government influences prices in some way. There are very few examples of a completely free market. It is also difficult to find examples of a completely controlled market. Even in the most rigorously planned economy, some market influences can usually be found.

Since there is no real-world example of a completely free market or a completely controlled market, the ambiguity of the preceding definitions need not generate much concern. All markets of economic interest lie on a continuum stretching between a theoretical free market and a theoretical controlled market. Since both ends of this continuum lie so far from any present market system, we are not in need of a definition that explicitly circumscribes the limits of the theoretical market types. It is important to determine the effects of public and private actions that move the market system closer to or farther from a system of administered prices; it is not important to quantify the distance from the pure forms of market control.

CORPORATE CONTROL OF MARKETS

So far this discussion has concentrated on government control of markets. However, market control is not exercised solely by government. Most examples of controlled markets are found in the actions of large corporations. This market control is often associated with the need for long-range planning, which in turn is necessitated by the large size generated by economies of scale. Thus the automobile manufacturers are said to require control over prices and quantities in order to organize the long and complex planning and organization required to develop and produce a new car design.[1]

The logic of the argument for market control follows the following general theme. Large firms cannot afford to subject their planned sales to the vagaries of a free market. Consumers must be persuaded to want the kind and quality of products generated by the resources that the planning processes committed to production at some prior time. Size requires planning, and planning permits and in fact requires the substitution of corporate control for market forces. Since consumer purchases in this planning environment are controlled by the supplier to fit the available supplies, the market no longer has a function to perform.

There is a fallacy in this line of thinking demonstrated quite clearly by events in the automobile industry in 1981. The automobile industry has been selected only for purposes of illustrating the relationship between firm size, long-range planning, and market control. The belief that corporate control is a natural alternative to market control as a capitalist society matures is based on the mistaken logic that market control is the natural outcome of long-range planning and that planning is the unique requirement of large firms. In fact, both large and small firms engage in planning. The time horizon varies with the ability of the manager, built-in lags in resource mobility, and the type of decision required. Size is neither a necessary nor a sufficient condition for long-range planning. For example, expansion of production

by individual small farmers often involves a planning horizon as long
as that required for designing a new car. A dairy farmer wishing to expand a herd will require at least three years to bring new calves into
production. Altering the genetic efficiency of the herd can easily require a lifetime, the planning is indeed complex, involving a large
number of other individuals, industries, and technologies. Long and
complex planning procedures are not unique to large corporations.

The connection between planning and market control is even
more tenuous. The preceding discussion has established that both
large and small firms engage in long-range planning. This leads to
market control only for the large firms. The difference between the
large and small firms is not their use of planning but their use of
market power. Both large and small firms have long and short planning horizons. Both "need" to control their market prices and final
demand to protect long-term investments in production resources and
technology. The difference between large and small firms is that the
large firm, having made a planning mistake, need not suffer the
market consequences. Its size provides it with four alternatives for
escaping the discipline of the market—alternatives that are not
generally available to the small firm. First, the firm can manipulate
consumer preference to persuade consumers to purchase the mistake at
a price that includes the cost of persuasion. Second, it can transfer
losses to another product from which market control can still generate
surplus profits. Third, it can exclude other firms (domestic or foreign)
from providing consumers with close substitutes, thereby guarantee-
ing a market for its own product. Fourth, it can use market influence
to generate political influence, creating protection from the consequences of planning mistakes.

If these four alternatives were completely effective, capitalism
would inevitably lead to the substitution of corporate control and
planning for market prices and market forces. However, all four of
these options have their limits. Even affluent consumers have a point
beyond which they will not respond to advertising. The market, in
terms of the demand curves of traditional economics, often reasserts
itself in an unexpected manner after a prolonged period of dormancy.
The impact is even more striking when years of consumer response
have created the illusion that consumer preferences are completely
under the control of the corporation's program of consumer persuasion.

Let us continue using the example of U.S. car manufacturers.

Their failure to read the consumers' preferences for small, economical cars was concealed for several years by a heavy advertising campaign to convince them that transportation was an expression of their personalities. When consumers lagged in their response to this advertising campaign, it became necessary to exclude foreign competition by "voluntary" import quotas (the third alternative discussed above). Ultimately it became necessary to use political influence to extract financial assistance from the taxpayers. The companies that were allowed to gain size and market power as a means to an efficient industry were now too large for government to allow them to suffer the consequences of planning mistakes. They had to be protected from the discipline of the market in order to remain "efficient." Consumers, as taxpayers, were required to provide financial assistance to the auto manufacturers who had been warning for years that it was not in the best interest of the American consumer to continue asking for small, fuel-efficient cars.

The auto industry, which for years exemplified the profitability of market control and consumer manipulation, found that corporate planning and market control cannot guarantee efficient and profitable operations unless the resulting economic power extends beyond persuasion to control of the consumers and alternative opportunities. I must conclude that the market is not outdated and has not outlived its role in an industrial society but has simply been excluded from many industries through the exercise of economic and political power. It is not my intent here to analyze control of the market by industrial corporations. The structure of American industry is far too complex to explore the transfer of market power from the consumer to the corporation within this treatise. The task has been ably done with far more rigor and documentation than I could hope to duplicate.[2] I prefer to turn my attention to control of the market through government policies.

GOVERNMENT CONTROL OF MARKETS

Since agriculture lacks the size and thus the power to substitute corporate control for market forces, government is increasingly interested in providing a means to this end. Government legislation and executive action are gradually substituting administrative decisions for the forces of supply and demand. The consequences of these actions on agriculture and on the food supply in the United States and the world are not well understood. Even worse, there is no well-organized system for evaluating the costs and benefits of individual policy actions.

Government policies in many countries have placed the market for every product somewhere along a continuum stretching between free markets and controlled markets. The exact location along the continuum differs among products, countries, and time periods. Daily actions in legislatures, courts, and regulatory agencies result in decisions that move those markets toward one or the other end of the continuum. The direction and magnitude of the movement not only differs among countries but is often reversed over time within the same country. An example of this can be found in Argentina, which operated within a free-market structure for more than a decade prior to 1974. In 1974 the responsibilities of the National Grain Board under the direction of the Junta Nacionale de Granos were expanded. It was designated as the sole legal market for all sales and purchases of Argentine grain. This government agency was also given responsibility for domestic and export prices and marketing margins.[3]

South Africa operates its industry through the Maize Board, a government monopoly enforced by law for the major maize-producing areas of the country. The board, operating toward the controlled-market end of the continuum, has made a small turn back toward the free market through deliberate policy decisions. In 1971 it removed price controls from the retail segment of the maize industry in response to a study that indicated competitition was sufficient to maintain price and income objectives without price controls at the retail level. The Livestock Control Board of South Africa is currently sponsoring a study to evaluate alternative strategies for improved marketing efficiency and responsiveness.

These examples illustrate the policy actions that often shift the market system along the continuum between free markets and administered prices. Recent examples from the U.S. experience illustrate similar shifts along the continuum, sometimes toward more and sometimes toward less control of the markets. The Grain Standards Act of 1976 authorized the newly created Federal Grain Inspection Service (FGIS) to replace all private inspection agencies with federal employees at export points. This action substituted a federal agency with power to determine prices for the private agencies that established prices for services based on supply and demand. The role of

FGIS in the grain industry continued to expand until the new Reagan philosophy succeeded in reducing the staff and the range of its responsibilities in 1981. According to the Associated Press, on October 18, 1981, FGIS dismissed nearly 25 percent of its staff. The work force was reduced from 1,216 to 945, and five regional field offices were closed. A three-year trend toward replacing private firms with government employees seems to have been halted if not reversed.

Bilateral agreements that specify maximum and minimum quantities of grain to be sold to certain nations have also increased in number and importance in the United States. These agreements add one more area from which market forces are excluded.

The preceding examples for the United States are small in terms of their individual economic impact. But their cumulative effect is to gradually shift the United States toward more reliance on government and less on market forces in establishing prices and quantities. As industry and the public become accustomed to the new position, additional increments are proposed. Since new policies are not part of an overall plan, the direction of cumulative effects is difficult to visualize. In general, the economic consequences of these individual policies are seldom identified, but their summation has clearly been to increase the role of government in agricultural markets. In a world of oil cartels and trade barriers, there is a certain appeal to the substitution of bureaucratic wisdom for the vagaries of the market in establishing prices and quantities, especially in the area of exports.

MEASURING THE EFFECTS OF GOVERNMENT MARKET CONTROL

The serious danger in suggested policy changes that would increase government's role in markets in all countries is the lack of analysis of the economic consequences of the alternatives. Most policies have been based on ideology rather than economic costs and benefits—partly because the economic analysis is seldom available, partly because it is difficult to incorporate economic criteria into political ideology, and partly because the parties involved have differing and often conflicting goals. How can these diverse policies and alternative actions be integrated into a systematic analysis of the economic consequences? We must first accept that it is not possible to compare total systems and conclude that the market-price system of Country A is superior (or inferior) to the administered-price system of

Country B. We cannot total all the pros and cons, take the algebraic sum, and identify a performance score for each system. Nor should we delude ourselves into thinking that the political system will do this for us and that it can best make the decisions. Neither the voters nor the politicians have a completely consistent set of values. Politicians generally do not try to develop a performance score for individual pieces of legislation, let alone for an entire complex marketing system. The Weaver Bill, introduced repeatedly in committee, has as its primary objective the creation of a government agency to establish minimum prices at which grain can be exported. This bill has not been promoted on the basis of the algebraic sum of its positive and negative benefits. When presented to farm audiences, it is promoted on the basis of its anticipated increase in farm prices. When it is presented to consumer audiences, it is promoted on the basis of more stable food prices. If the bill is argued before the administration or the secretary of agriculture, its positive impact on foreign trade is highlighted. Most issues are debated and decided on one criterion or a very few criteria at a time, and seldom is there any attempt to calculate a weighted algebraic-sum type of index.

The evaluation of free versus controlled markets makes sense only if we examine small pieces of the system rather than the totality. In addition, the evaluation of the small pieces must be made individually, using one criterion at a time. There is no quantitative way to add a little more stability to a considerable decrease in competition and arrive at a meaningful quantitative net welfare effect. The contribution economists make to evaluation of performance is to help identify the trade-offs in the various policy alternatives. The question is not whether greater stability can compensate for lesser income but whether the stability can be achieved only by reduced income.

There is one additional problem that has frustrated economists in their attempts to measure performance. Most authors have used either perfect competition as a quantitative norm or a qualitative distance from a quantitative norm. For example, Sosnick (1968) identified twenty-five market characteristics, any one of which disqualified a market as effectively competitive. However, most of these characteristics were described in qualitative terms such as "needlessly dangerous" and "unjustified profits."[4] The alternative to quantification on a cardinal scale is a comparative evaluation against a specific alternative on a single variable. It is much easier to determine that policy A decreases price variability relative to policy B than it is to establish that policy A results in "unacceptable" levels of price variability. The ultimate purpose of measuring performance is to advise policymakers of the economic consequences (costs and benefits) of alternative policies. The impact of policy A on price variability can be given a comparative ranking with an alternative policy. It is an unacceptable policy only if there is a better alternative that can be instituted. A free market in the pure sense is not a viable alternative and is therefore not a relevant standard for comparision.

The evaluative procedure that I am suggesting proceeds as follows. First, a policy action such as the Weaver Bill is separated into the specific marketing functions that will be affected. For example, one section of the Weaver proposal would replace the market price for grain exports with a government agency empowered to establish prices in accordance with international policies and political objectives, with explicit recognition of the trade policies of major buyers in the European Community and other countries.

The second step in my evaluation procedure is to identify the criteria on which the policy should be judged. Although there is some degree of subjectivity in establishing criteria, it is fairly easy to obtain agreement on some of the most important ones. Continuing with the example of the Weaver Bill, it is clear that most people are interested in the effects of the bill on efficiency, price level and stability, response to changing demand and supply, and incentives. There are other criteria, and some on the list could be subdivided, but this will suffice for the present illustrative discourse.

The third step in the evaluation is the most difficult. We must analyze the ability of the policy to move us closer to or farther away from each of the performance goals implied by our criteria. The intent is not to measure the distance from our position to the ideal but only to determine if the action under consideration moves us closer than a selected alternative to the controlled market on one end of the continuum or to the free market on the other. We are comparing incremental movements by direction, not by magnitude, and thus need no clear quantification of absolute goals. It is sufficient to establish that the Weaver Bill would produce greater price stability than our current export market system; we need not concern ourselves with measuring absolute price stability nor determine if price stability is good or bad.

Since economists seldom have the luxury of organizing controlled experiments, the empirical comparison of two alternative procedures for directing U.S. grain exports must be limited to a comparison across countries or over very long time periods within a country. Both of these techniques are subject to the dangers of leaving important variables outside the scope of the study. Nonetheless, the approach can shed some light on the problem and provide supplemental support to an analysis based on theory or ideology.

Since we have started with the example of government control of export quantities and prices, let us follow through by comparing the U.S. grain export system with that of a country already operating with a government agency in charge of grain exports. Since Canada produces with similar resources, sells into the same international markets, and uses similar physical facilities for assembly and distribution, a comparison of the Canadian Wheat Board and the U.S. market-oriented exporting firms enables us to draw some conclusions about relative performance.

I shall illustrate my evaluation procedures by comparing the U.S. and Canadian systems on a selected set of criteria. To rank these criteria or goals is not my objective. I shall evaluate both systems on four important criteria: efficiency, price level and stability, response to changing demand and supply, and incentives.

Efficiency. Efficiency will be used to mean performance of the basic marketing functions at the lowest possible resource cost. This includes development and use of cost-saving technologies. The market system enforces operating efficiency because the inefficient are unable to compete. Quantitative measures of efficiency are difficult to obtain. A study of the U.S. and Canadian wheat marketing systems shows that marketing costs, excluding transportation, were 70.1 cents per bushel in Canada and 40.4 cents per bushel in the United States for performing essentially the same marketing function for equivalent quality, geographic areas, and export destinations during the period 1974–1979.[5] Two additional studies of the U.S. and Canadian systems concluded that Canadian technological development was lagging behind that of the United States in the areas of transportation, export facilities, and grain handling.[6,7] Although the discipline of the market appears to increase efficiency, the private costs of investment losses due to financial failure should not be ignored. "Survival of the fittest" is an effective method of increasing efficiency, but it imposes individual losses, adjustment hardships, and the social cost of investment mistakes. Efficiency is achieved at a cost, but we are examining only one criterion at a time and the market provides an advantage in terms of operational efficiency.

Price Level and Price Stability. The role of price in a market economy is to allocate goods among competing consumers and resources among competing production alternatives. In the absence of free-market prices other methods of allocation must be employed, for consumers' desires always exceed the available supply of goods. Even in an economy of administered prices, the quality of goods consumed and the mix of consumer items selected is determined by consumer incomes and personal preferences as well as the relative prices of all goods. Allocation of goods can be made by government decree, rationing, or prices, but in all cases goods and people must be matched.

Despite the frequent argument that marketing boards increase farm prices, there is little supporting evidence if we look at countries such as Canada, which have traditionally used marketing boards. A comparison of actual price data between 1973-1974 and 1978-1979 provides no evidence that Canada has been able to sell its grain at higher prices or that it has paid any consistent premium to its producers. Canada's export price after adjustment for quality and moisture closely follows that of the United States. Both countries are selling to the same buyers, who are trying to buy at the lowest price. Canada's export price was above the U.S. price in 1973, 1977, and 1978 but below the U.S. price in 1974, 1975, and 1976.[8] Farm prices have shown a similar pattern. U.S. farm prices were above Canada's in crop years 1974 and 1975, below in 1977 and 1978, and equal in 1976.

In addition to the interest in price levels, consumers and producers are interested in price stability. Prices are highly volatile in the United States, shifting from season to season in accordance with demand and supply. Since a marketing board establishes prices for producers, there is no doubt that day-to-day, week-to-week, and month-to-month prices vary less under a marketing board system than under a free-market system. Chicago Board of Trade prices vary every minute. Wide swings in prices with the accompanying profits and losses are not a possibility under a board system such as Canada's in which the producers are all paid the same base price averaged out over the entire year's sales.

Response to Changing Demand and Supply. A market-oriented system is composed of millions of individuals making price and quantity decisions minute by minute. With their livelihood dependent on the quality of these decisions, response is rapid. Even small price differences will shift thousands of tons of grain among destinations in a matter of days. The complex system of assembling, storing, and transporting is tied together by an instantaneous chain of price information. Consequently, an increase in exports of U.S. wheat and wheat products from 17.7 million tons in 1970 to 37.6 million tons in 1980 was absorbed into the transportation system through thousands of grain elevators with no central planners to select the ports, transport modes, and farm origins. Similar response is seldom seen in planned economies where logistics and capacities are directed from a central office and plans and goals are often thwarted by unresponsive logistical systems.

A review of the market shares in Canada and the United States since 1965 illustrates the response problems. Whenever world demand increased and total world imports took an upward swing, Canada's share of the world market declined and the U.S. share increased. When world demand declined below the trend line, Canada's share increased and the U.S. share decreased. Canada increased its market share in periods of relatively low world prices. Marketing board systems and planned economies often have difficulty responding to fluctuating demand and new opportunities as markets grow and increase. The determination of who takes the larger share of the market is primarily a function of the ability of the exporting system and producers of the country to respond to changes in demand.

Incentives. One of the primary areas of concern regarding incentives is the production response to increases in domestic and world demand. Using the pricing system to redistribute wealth or as a device for maintaining income equity among all members of an economic sector frequently reduces individual incentives. The Canadian and U.S. cereal growers have had yields that grow consistently higher each year than those of most other countries. Much of this is due to more favorable growing conditions. But as McCalla and Schmitz point out, "policy also influences yields and the associated production cost."[9] The incentives and opportunity for individual profits have given the United States a historical problem with overproduction and oversupply. It thus becomes very difficult to say whether the controlled economy or the free market is more efficient. But in terms of production response, the data seem to indicate that the free market has a clear advantage. The Soviet model of control planning has had problems in stimulating production. Although the Union of Soviet Socialist Republics (USSR) is self-sufficient in food grains, it requires extensive imports of cereals to support a growing livestock industry demanded by consumers. The problem of incentives in the USSR and in the planned economies in general was pointed out by former Premier Nikita Khrushchev (1974) in his memoirs. "Unfortunately material incentive hasn't been used much as an instrument to spur agricultural production. Compensation for collective farmers has only in small part been determined by their productivity. I realize that by publicly advocating material incentives, I'm opening myself up to those know-it-alls who will say our people should be motivated not by money but by ideological considerations. That's nonsense. I'm old enough to know from experience that the majority of collective farm administrators who are paid a flat salary won't take any chances for the sake of improving production."[10]

Based on the comparison of U.S. and Canadian grain marketing systems, one can conclude that the substitution of administrative decision making for market forces in world markets for grain will increase price stability, decrease marketing efficiency, decrease resource responsiveness, and have little effect on price levels. These conclusions cannot be generalized, but they serve to illustrate the comparison of alternative policies on a limited set of economic criteria. The comparisons leave unanswered the question of whether increased price stability is worth the cost of reduced responsiveness to market opportunities. It also excludes questions not generally answered by economists, such as, What will be the political repercussions in terms of trade negotiations or the ability of less developed countries to purchase supplies in high-priced markets? Perhaps the findings can be stated more confidently and generalized by restating the conclusions. Substitution of a government marketing agency for the U.S. market system will not guarantee higher prices to producers or increased efficiency in the industry. A comparison of various marketing systems around the world demonstrates that an administered price system is neither sufficient nor necessary to improve performance in U.S. grain markets. Proponents of increasing the role of government in U.S. agricultural markets cannot base their case on assurances of improved prices, increased marketing efficiency, or responsiveness to opportunities in world markets. There are no examples in the grain industry to support this position.

An evaluation of policy alternatives affecting agricultural markets should clearly specify the set of criteria on which the evaluation is based and should identify quantifiable variables that when measured will relate to those criteria. The narrower the focus and the fewer the variables under study, the greater will be the probability of a generalized conclusion. Most market systems are extremely complex and inextricably intertwined with the economic and political systems of the country. This warrants repetition of my earlier statement that we cannot select one system as "good" and another as "bad" because of the difficulty of aggregating the many diverse objectives and ideologies that interact to establish and alter the market system. This does not, however, give the economist license to ignore the nonquantifiable or macroeconomic variables.

CONCLUSIONS

Agricultural markets do not operate in isolation from the rest of the economy but do so within a much larger sphere of domestic and foreign policies and influences. These relationships dictate and circumscribe the range of alternatives available to market participants. Although changes in industry structure can alter market performance, many such opportunities lie outside the industry in the economic, political, and regulatory environment. Inflation, unemployment, interest rates, and fiscal policy exert important influences on the organization and performance of agricultural markets. Cyclical enforcement of antitrust policies alternately encourage and discourage corporate growth. Policies to alter historical patterns of distribution of income and wealth also influence the operation of markets. Freely operating markets do not meet many of the social and political goals deemed important. Consequently, government involvement through legislation and regulation becomes an acceptable and important substitute for the market forces of competition.

The economic and political influences on U.S. agricultural markets are not restricted to U.S. policies. Importing and exporting nations establish domestic and trade policies that have direct bearing on U.S. markets. Fluctuating exchange rates among the currencies of the world are correlated with purchases of U.S. grains. The actions of the Organization of Petroleum Exporting Countries (OPEC) have not only altered economic relationships for agriculture but have generated a new attitude among farmers wanting to emulate the success of OPEC with a system of controlled prices and international grain cartels. Agricultural markets influence economic and political decisions and are in turn influenced by nearly every event throughout the world.

The complexity of evaluating the effects of alternative policies on market performance tempts us to abandon the effort. But yielding to that temptation permits the cumulative effects of policy changes over time to move our market system along the continuum in a direction we would not have chosen had we been able to list the long-range effects in total. There are objectives of society that cannot be achieved through a free-market system. Attempts by government bodies to use the market to meet these objectives not only distort resource use and reduce economic incentives but often fail to move the economy toward the original goal. A better understanding of the role of the market in society and the role of government in the market can improve the performance of both.

The ideas and frustrations that surfaced during the development of this discussion have led me to a basic question for agricultural economists not only in the United States but in every country of the world. What is the proper role of government with respect to agricultural markets? Without a clear answer, policy direction has the appearance of a random-walk strategy and will move very slowly if at all toward increased welfare for consumers or producers. Clearly the answer is not simple. Well-informed and well-intentioned people will often disagree. The need for reviewing diverse views from multiple foci generated the idea for the chapters that follow. They reflect diverse points of view on how public policy can or should be used in improving performance of the markets for agriculture. These six lectures are given within the broad context of market performance. The criteria used for evaluation are often implicit but nonetheless real, and each author clearly employs a different set of performance criteria and norms against which to measure the success of government and industry.

NOTES

1. J. K. Galbraith, *The New Industrial State,* 3rd ed., rev. (Boston: Houghton Mifflin, 1978), p. 197.
2. Ibid., p. 34.
3. U.S. General Accounting Office, *"Grain Marketing Systems in Argen-*

tina, Australia, Canada, and the European Community; Soybean Marketing Systems in Brazil, Report of the Comptroller General of the United States, May 28, 1976, p. 6.

4. Stephen H. Sosnick, "Toward a Concrete Concept of Effective Competition," *American Journal of Agricultural Economics* 50(Nov. 1968): 827–51.

5. N. L. Dollinger, *Comparative Analysis of Transport and Handling of Export Wheat in Canada and the U.S.* M.S. Thesis, University of Illinois, Urbana, 1981.

6. Alex McCalla and Andrew Schmitz, "Grain Marketing Systems: The Case of the United States vs. Canada," *American Journal of Agricultural Economics* 61(May 1979):199–212.

7. Keith Peltier and Donald W. Anderson, "The Canadian Grain Marketing System," Agric. Econ. Rep. 130, North Dakota State University, Fargo, 1978.

8. Dollinger, *Analysis of Transport.*

9. McCalla and Schmitz, "Grain Marketing Systems."

10. Nikita S. Khrushchev, *Khrushchev Remembers: The Last Testament* (Boston: Little, Brown, 1974).

3

Change and the Economy

J O H N   K .   G A L B R A I T H

IN the twenty-five years following World War II, there was great, sometimes exuberant satisfaction with economic performance in the industrial countries. Capitalism, to the surprise even of some of its exponents, was a success. The crises and depressions that had marked its history over the previous 100 years—first, confidence and euphoria then depression, unemployment, and despair—seemed under control. Output during these two and one-half decades increased steadily. From 1946 (the first peacetime year) through 1969, there was only one year when the real gross national product in the United States showed an appreciable decline and only two in which it failed to register a substantial advance. Performance in the other industrial countries was generally as good; in Japan and Germany it was much better.

The expansion in output kept unemployment low and, with all else, prices were stable. In 1948, by which time the wartime distortions had been mostly worked off, the U.S. index of wholesale prices (1967 = 100) was at 83; two decades later the index stood at 102.5. This increase of less than twenty percentage points in twenty years would not now be considered astonishing if it took place in one.

As prices in these twenty years were stable, so, in general, were the international exchanges. From time to time there was a sterling crisis, which involved the failure to achieve a wholly fixed relationship between the pound and the dollar and the pound and other currencies. On occasion, usually after much wringing of well-manicured hands, other countries adjusted the value of their currency in relation to the dollar. What was then thought a dangerous departure from

John K. Galbraith is Paul M. Warburg Professor of Economics Emeritus at Harvard University, Cambridge, Mass.

stable exchange rates would now be considered unbelievable reliability.

During these years, governments of varying complexion were in power in the various industrial countries—Republicans and Democrats in the United States and Labour and Conservatives in Great Britain. The Social Democrats dominated in Scandinavia; the Christian Socialists, in the process of giving way to the Social Democrats, were in power in Germany and Austria; Gaullists and others of slightly varying shades held office in France; and the conservative Liberal Democrats dominated the scene in Japan. Clearly the political complexion of governments, or the changes therein, had little to do with economic well-being. Conservatives saw in this period proof of the perfectibility of capitalism and the free enterprise system; American liberals saw it as the triumph of Keynes and the mixed economy; and to Social Democrats it showed the wisdom of a well-considered intervention by the state in strategic areas and a widening concern for social welfare. So it was until nearly the end of the 1960s. Then the good years came to an end.

All things must be kept in perspective. The economic difficulties of the 1970s have not matched in misfortune the disaster of the Great Depression. By the spring of 1933, three and one-half years after the climactic crash in the New York stock market, a quarter of the U.S. labor force was unemployed. There was no unemployment insurance and no organized welfare system. By this time 9,000 American banks had failed without the cushion of deposit insurance. Hundreds of thousands of other firms had gone bankrupt, including the very large national and utility combines. The debts of American farmers by the mid-1930s exceeded their assets at current values. Not until 1937 did the physical volume of output recover to the 1929 level. In 1938 one worker in five was still without employment.

The United States and Germany were two of the worst cases. These were the two countries, it is worth recalling, with the leaders— Herbert Hoover in the United States and Heinrich Breuning in Germany—who were thought to be the soundest in their economic views and most committed to orthodox and accepted principles. But economic life in all the industrial countries in these years was very grim. By comparison with the Great Depression, the recent experience is with a crisis of prosperity.

Still, by the 1970s things were no longer going well, and problems continue. Unemployment has been persistently higher than in the earlier postwar decades. Inflation (Germany, Austria, and Switzerland apart) has become a major preoccupation and a source of much anxiety and distress. International exchanges have shown a magnitude of fluctuation that would once have been thought inconceivable. The dollar, since World War II the accepted *numéraire* for all international calculations, has been uniquely unreliable.

What has gone wrong? And what chance is there of things going right? Or, as I would prefer, of being made to go right?

ECONOMICS AND HISTORICAL CHANGE

Let me urge, if only as an experiment, that we seek to answer these questions without undue recourse to political self-indulgence. The opposite, alas, is our habit. We all dislike paying taxes; almost automatically we say that oppressive taxation is the cause of our difficulties. Unions are often inconvenient, so all difficulties are attributed to organized labor. Public regulation is often unpleasant, so all fault is attributed to efforts to protect the environment or get more gasoline mileage from automobiles. Gasoline being expensive or occasionally scarce, all economic ills are attributed to the Organization of Petroleum Exporting Countries (OPEC) or to the great oil companies. I attended a meeting called by senior Washington leaders to consider the problems of energy and inflation. The remedies offered were all in accordance with what the prescribing individual found most profitable or convenient to believe. The business executives came out strongly for more pollution and after-tax profits as the solution for the energy shortage and inflation. The economists, having no cure for either, united in predicting a recession, for which they could prescribe tax reductions (to general applause).

In economic discussion the most dangerous form of self-indulgence, verging on romanticism, is to imagine there is a known set of economic rules that were once observed and have now been abandoned. Economic life must be guided by these rules. Live by them, recapture the commitment to eighteenth-century fundamentals, and all will be well. This was the promise of Raymond Barre in France, Margaret Thatcher in Great Britain, and Menachem Begin in Israel. In making this effort, all managed to enhance the rate of inflation and the level of unemployment.

The great and immutable truth is that economic institutions and economic life are in a continuous process of change. This change is much more rapid and persistent than economists, yearning for the solidity of scientific truth and resisting the obsolescence of their textbooks, ever wish to concede. The modern corporation, in its increasing scale, changing internal structure, and agglomerative tendency, is such a force for change, but not precisely an invisible one. So are work habits. So are changes in consumer taste and behavior as people are released from their erstwhile occupational commitments to particular habits in food, shelter, clothing, and other basic needs. So is the changing role of the state.

Change cannot be stopped or reversed. Only in the romantic dreams of American liberals can corporate growth and concentration be arrested by law. Only in hope and oratory will government regulation be abandoned in increasingly interdependent societies. In the United States there has been a deafening outburst of oratory attacking burdensome, unnecessary, and crippling regulation. A great chorus of voices demands that government get off the backs of the people. This has been accompanied by a nearly unprecedented demand for more and better government regulation and intervention. When a DC-10 airplane crashed, there were demands for tighter airline regulation; following the accident at Three Mile Island, there were demands for much more comprehensive regulation of nuclear power; as the Chrysler Corporation neared collapse, there came demands that the U.S. government (like those of Great Britain, France, Italy, and Germany) get involved in the automobile business. These demands have come from precisely the people who are most critical of government regulation—the affluent friends of free enterprise.

It is to historical imperative, not ideology, that economic policy must respond. It follows that policy must be a continuous adaptation to change. Here is the beginning of the explanation of our economic difficulties now and in earlier times. Economic policy regularly lags behind compelling historical change. This happened in the Great Depression. It had long been an article of economic faith that an economic system could not suffer a shortage of demand (purchasing power). Economists remained committed to the great but obsolete theorem of Jean Baptiste Say that the production and sale of a good always paid out the requisite demand. So they resisted proposals for deliberate expansion of purchasing power by the state, urged balanced budgets, and warned against easy money and other economic experiments. And so urging, they went into the dustbin of history, if one can borrow from Lenin. We can understand our present difficulties only if we realize that there has been further great change in economic life and that economists and economic policy have been lagging resolutely behind. I deal first with the changes, then with the consequences of our failure to respond, and finally with the needed response.

CHANGES IN ECONOMIC LIFE

Decline in Worker Productivity. In the industrial countries, the changes to which economic policy has not adapted are, at a minimum, three. They are highly visible; and once they are mentioned, few will deny their importance.

The first of these changes, one accepted only with the utmost reluctance, is in work habits. With industrial maturity and increasing affluence, people simply like hard work less and work less hard. So worker productivity declines. The effect is greatest in plants characterized by simple, tedious, repetitive toil—textile mills, automobile assembly lines, crude steel manufacture, shipbuilding. It is least where tasks are varied, interesting, innovative, that is, intellectually or artistically demanding.

That economic development is accompanied by rejection of tedious work should occasion no surprise. For years, scholars with a reputation for social foresight (when otherwise devoid of subject) have told of the coming age of leisure. Above a certain level of income, people have always rejected hard toil; the rich have long been called the leisure class. What is called the work ethic has always been thought exceptionally ethical for the poor. Those who have never experienced hard toil have always been indignant over the casual tendencies of those who have. We must now assume that with increasing well-being, people will be less inclined to heavy, continuous routine. There is no British disease and no emerging American disease. There are only differences in industrial age.

It follows that the effect of changing work attitudes on productivity will vary in different countries depending on age. In Japan it will be less marked than in Great Britain and the United States. However, even older Japanese industries are beginning to feel the pressure from the more eager textile and shipbuilding workers of South Korea and Taiwan.

The impact will also be different to the extent that foreign workers or immigrants are used. Germany, France, Switzerland, and to some extent Austria have been able to delay the productivity effect by bringing in workers from Yugoslavia, Italy, Spain, and Portugal. For them, industrial work is more attractive in terms of effort and much more attractive in terms of income than the harsh rural existence previously experienced. Detroit and other northern American cities have survived by getting successive drafts of workers from rural areas— first from the southern Appalachians and then from the Deep South. Some countries have resisted. The English automobile industry staggers from crisis to crisis because it makes automobiles (though by no means exclusively) with English labor. The German automobile firms would be in equally deep trouble were they to make automobiles with German labor.

Investment and trade union practices also have their effect on productivity. We must now assume that productivity will decline in the older, relatively labor-intensive industries such as steel, textiles, and shipbuilding. It is the first of the historical imperatives to which we must accommodate with something other than speeches deploring the fecklessness of the working classes.

Breakdown of Consumption Limits.   The breakdown of occupational limits on consumption is the second great change—the second historical imperative. It is also a natural consequence of affluence and the spread of democratic attitudes and ethos. Something must also be attributed to education and television. In all the industrial countries there was once a blue-collar standard of living; a somewhat higher white-collar standard; a professional standard; and a standard that was deemed appropriate to the property-owning, entrepreneurial, and privileged classes. Access to education, travel, and health care were all appropriate to class, as were housing, dress, and forms of recreation.

Large occupational differences in living standards remain, but they are no longer held to be natural, prescriptive, or uniquely appropriate to class or occupation. The son and daughter of a working-class family are assumed to have a right to attend a university. Their jeans are not readily distinguishable except by a fashion expert from those of the children of the employer. Even in the United States (a retarded case) there is a persistent feeling that everyone should have access to a doctor. No one, of course, can be denied a car. Travel is increasingly assumed to be the right of all.

Again there are differences between the old countries and the new. The class identity in consumption standards is stronger in Japan than in the United States, although it is not so strong as to deny any Japanese a charter flight to San Francisco or Paris or, as one views Tokyo traffic, an automobile.

This release of consumption from occupational and class restraint has powerful economic effects. In particular, it puts strong pressure on the supply of private and public goods and services. When backed by the requisite purchasing power (that is, effective demand), it can easily press beyond the productive capacity of the economy at current prices. In so doing, it becomes a strong force for inflation. A reduction in such demand to restrain inflation no longer involves curtailment of consumption, public or private, by either a limited and privileged class or a larger but voiceless mass. In restraining demand to prevent inflation, a modern democratic government must now act against the increasingly democratic consumption habits of its people. This is not politically attractive.

Escape from Market Authority. The third of the historical changes is the growing successful effort of increasingly strong organizations in the economy to escape the authority of the market and gain control over their prices and income and thus over their levels of consumption. Control of income and associated benefits is the purpose of the trade union, and in conjunction with the state such control is the *raison d'être* of the farm organization. No industrial country now leaves its farm prices to the market; when farmers dislike their prices, they no longer assail the buyers of their products. They turn their wrath on the government. The minimum wage now protects those who have no union from the market. The artist, scientist, and business executive, all increasingly important in economic life, have the bargaining power that goes with talent. We recognize this in the common commendatory expression, ''he can name his own price.''

Control of prices and customer response (to the greatest extent possible) are also basic to all modern corporate planning. This is the *raison d'être* of the modern great corporation. It would be reckless to spend hundreds of millions of dollars on a new automobile model

without some assurance as to its eventual price or some effort to ensure
that people will want it.

When the OPEC countries came together to control the price of
the world's most important raw material, it was widely thought to be
something new—an economic development of its own kind. We see it
now in proper perspective. OPEC is part of the historical process in
which the authority of the market gives way to the authority of
organization, that is, to the power of those who sell or, less frequently,
the power of those who buy.

OPEC has seemed exceptional because the assertion of power over
oil prices was sudden and the magnitude of change great and because
the industrial world in general and the United States in particular have
made such a massive economic, social, and cultural adjustment to in-
expensive oil. The automobile population; the suburbanization of
cities; supermarkets, shopping centers, and shopping habits; travel
and recreation; automatic furnaces; even the prestige structure
associated with the size and cost of the motor vehicle are all part of this
adjustment to cheap oil. OPEC also seemed exceptional because such
exercise of power by Third World countries was not expected. General
Motors and Volkswagen have long controlled the price of their
products; the need for certainty and the most remunerative return is
assumed. The better the return, the better things are. For the Saudis
to behave as they have was a surprise.

Having achieved control over their incomes, organizations and individuals in the industrial countries have inevitably sought to increase
them. These efforts are enhanced by the breakdown of old occupational limits on living standards. What some have, others now assume
they should have as well. The result is a further upward pressure on
prices, wages, and salaries—a second major cause of inflation.

Of the three changes, this last is the most visible and the one that
encounters the greatest intellectual resistance. This is partly because
business people have been told always to say they are subordinate to
the market in all they do. Nothing is thought more improper than to
admit to the power to raise prices. In the United States it is even legally dangerous; lawyers warn their clients against careless resort to truth.
Many otherwise distinguished economists have strongly and often in-
dignantly rejected the notion of corporate, trade union, farm, and
other organized power as a cause of rising prices, that is, inflation.
Such recognition accepts that prices and incomes reflect the organized

power of sellers. This diminishes the role of the market and undercuts the subject matter of economics as it is taught. So, faced with a change that is rendering their lecture notes, textbooks, and public advice obsolete, one large group of economists have not hesitated. They have denied that any change has taken place.

ACCOMMODATIONS TO CHANGE

The three changes mentioned above tell us what has gone wrong with modern economic policy and, more by force of circumstances than by force of thought, about the accommodation to historical process that is needed to make the policy more nearly right.

These changes tell us why Japan and the yet newer countries have an advantage in the labor-intensive industries. They tell us why, having encouraged economic development, we now find, rather to our surprise, that developing countries have cloth, steel, shoes, and other products to sell at prices we cannot meet. They also tell why foreign labor or drafts of workers fresh from the farm in all industrial countries in the postwar years have been so important. They suggest, more than incidentally, that the industrial countries should have a more functional view of immigration and that they can greatly help themselves by welcoming people who, fortunately, want to come. The experience of Germany, Austria, and Switzerland also shows that such immigration can be quite undamaging to the domestic trade union position.

The changing attitudes toward industrial work and the consequences for labor productivity tell us that the economic future of the older industrial countries lies in industries with a high input of intellectual, scientific, or artistic talent. In the United States and Western Europe such industries (Danish furniture, Paris and New York clothing, unlistenable American records, books universally) survive all competition—so on the whole do computers and aircraft.

The release of consumption from its occupational restraints and the resulting pressure for public and private services give us the first of the causes of inflation. These factors also tell us of the difficulty that modern governments have in using fiscal policy (that is, higher taxes and lower public spending) to control aggregate demand. Such policy encounters the widely distributed and articulated pressure to bring lower living standards abreast of the higher ones. Politicians are regularly held to be craven for their failure to counter this pressure for higher private and especially higher public consumption. The need now is for more bravery than commonly imagined.

Mass-consumption pressures also explain another shortcoming in modern economic management. Not wishing to challenge public or private consumption, governments fall back on monetary policy. This (restriction on spending from bank lending) requires no legislation. It is also not quite understood by legislators or the public. Because of their generally good manners and tailoring, central bankers are widely supposed to be the repositories of special insight allowing the exercise of some special magic. Because we all respect money, we cannot help thinking that its proper management will somehow solve all our ills.

Monetary policy is the great illusion of our time. If it worked (that is, if it could maintain stable prices without serious unemployment) some country somewhere would have learned its secret long before now.

Monetary policy works against inflation only as it creates slack in the economy, causing idle plant capacity and unemployment, that is, a recession. Only when a recession is serious will trade unions, other organized groups, and strong corporations be restrained. All recent experience verifies this. Monetary policy also singles out for special punishment the firm that depends on borrowed money because such policy works by restricting borrowing and spending. It does not similarly affect the firm that can invest from its own earnings or pass along its higher interest costs in higher prices. Tight money does not hurt the big corporations much; it can have a brutal effect on housing, agriculture, small merchants, and other small businesses. This too is borne out by history.

A further difficulty with monetary policy is that no one knows the relation between any given act of monetary restraint and the consequence. That is why in all the industrial countries we have such repetitious and banal discussion over whether a given tightening of money rates portends a recession or a depression, and it is why such predictions regularly turn out to be wrong. There is a rational case against excessive reliance on any instrument of policy for which the results are so uncertain.

Finally, at a time when there is a deep concern in the industrial countries over productivity and when nothing can be done to counter the cultural tendencies of a maturing working force, it is foolish to curb excess demand by cutting back selectively on investment. That is what monetary policy does. It means that as workers work less hard, we do not compensate by investing in better equipment. We aggravate the problem of productivity by deliberately cutting back on investment.

An effective attack on inflation still requires control of adequate demand. Since the present reliance on monetary policy is unacceptable, only fiscal policy (that is, tax or expenditure adjustment) remains. This has its primary effect, not on investment, but on consumption. The results are more predictable. Difficult or not, it must be used.

One way of easing the difficulty is to make greater use of indirect taxation on upper-income expenditure. This taxation can no longer be by item; clothing, vehicles, and even food, depending on cost, can be the greatest of essentials or the greatest of luxuries. Such taxes must be graded in their impact on the cost of the item. Having a selective impact on what are still called luxuries, such taxation is politically more feasible. Unlike the income tax, no case can be made against it on incentive grounds. It should now come in for much greater use.

Fiscal policy also works against the price-setting power of corporations, trade unions, and farmers only as it causes unemployment, creates slack, and induces recession. This result is wanted no more than inflation. To ease the task of fiscal policy, there must also be direct intervention to manage prices and incomes. Where the organized power of corporations and unions has replaced the authority of the market, there must be a policy for prices and incomes of individual firms. This policy does not make it less necessary to control demand using fiscal policy. It lessens the need for unemployment and industrial slack to achieve the same result.

In Germany, Austria, Switzerland, and Scandinavia the trade unions have come to accept the fact that increases in money income must be consistent with current price levels. Industry- and country-wide bargaining have aided in this effort. The need to match external prices has helped to hold prices in line, as has development of an understanding that wage restraint must be matched by price and profit restraints. In Japan the problem of wage/price inflation is eased by industrial growth, high productivity, and a close working association between government, trade unions, and corporations. In Great Britain and the United States, governments are still struggling to develop a more formal system of restraint—a consensus on an income and price policy. There is no escape that does not involve either recession or inflation as the alternative. When God imposed these unpleasant choices on economic policymakers, he left himself open to criticism.

My American economic colleagues are gradually coming to accept the inevitable. Jimmy Carter's economists arrived in Washington convinced that God was a Keynesian Democrat. They said that there would be no price or wage guidelines and no controls. However, wage and price guidelines were soon introduced and enforced by voluntary methods, something of a contradiction in terms. Firm controls on large employers and major trade union contracts are no longer ruled out by anyone with nontheological instinct.

The development of such direct restraint is the greatest current task in the accommodation of economic thought and policy to underlying economic change. It is the modern counterpart of the great Keynesian accommodation of forty years ago, but a more difficult one. The Keynesian accommodation propped up the economy and allowed income and price determinations (the market) to function as before. The present accommodation must compensate for the failure of the market itself.

As noted, the accommodation of policy to the decline of the market is proceeding at different rates in different countries. Japan, a young country with high labor productivity and an amenable labor force, is the easiest case. Germany, with an advanced view of the problem of restraining incomes, its long-standing fear of inflation, the requisite organization and discipline of its trade unions, and its accepted recourse to foreign labor, is also a relatively easy case. Both Germany and Japan are also mastering the problems created by OPEC's new market control of oil. The accommodation to the decline of the market and the rise of organized income- and price-setting power will continue to be much slower and more difficult in Great Britain and the United States.

Because of its high and uncontrolled consumption, the United States has a particularly difficult problem accommodating to OPEC control of oil prices. Part of the answer is to get our domestic inflation under control. As the experiences of Germany and Japan show, that is one way of getting oil imports under control as well. But we also need to limit imports directly, with a companion decision to live with what is available. This will require an elementary system for rationing motor fuel; we cannot do it all by price without a punishing effect on the poor. In the absence of such control, dollars will continue to accumulate in foreign hands and will continue, like the Bedouins, to move from one camping ground to another, bidding up Swiss francs and German marks, bidding down the dollar, and perpetuating currency instability. Nothing would more directly serve currency stability (the stability of the dollar) than control of oil imports and a reduction in our oil deficit.

CONCLUSIONS

Such are our circumstances and the prospect before us. The latter is not entirely dark. It will be brighter if we see that accommodation to change is normal. It would be brighter still, and business people and politicians might be happier, if they could see it as an interesting adventure. It is not clear as to why economic change must always be discussed with a commitment to morbid gloom. As I have said, it is the deepest conviction of both neoclassical conservatives and believing Marxists that capitalism functions only within firmly ordained rules; ignore those rules and it falters or collapses. Fortunately, this is not true. The experience of the last half-century shows that capitalism lends itself to an infinity of pragmatic patching-up. If it did not, it would have perished long ago.

4

Social Control of Private Economic Power

WILLARD F. MUELLER

THE CASE FOR SOCIAL CONTROL

The predominant and distinguishing characteristic of our economic system is that it is run largely by private businesses. These enterprises range in size from small shopkeepers, farmers, and providers of numerous services to enormous corporations whose individual revenues eclipse those of most nations. I shall address the role played in our economy by these large corporations.

Large corporations have been given the responsibility of running key sectors of our economy. For the most part, they process and distribute our food, make our transportation equipment, control our financial system, manufacture the armaments needed for national defense, hold commanding positions in most other important industries, and are leading economic participants in many nations throughout the world. Business historian Harold Livesay explains that private corporations have been appointed the chief caretakers of the American dream of universal prosperity and happiness.[1] Harold Geneen, former chairman of International Telephone and Telegraph (ITT), takes for granted that the larger corporations have become the primary custodians of making our entire system work.[2]

Few would quarrel with the view that large corporations are the custodians of our economic machine. They have much to say about the

Willard F. Mueller is William F. Vilas Research Professor of Agricultural Economics, Professor of Economics, and Professor in the Law School, University of Wisconsin, Madison.

nature and timing of capital investments, the character and quality of the products we consume, the volume and direction of research and development effort, and other matters that affect the quality of our lives.

A few statistics illustrate the extent and growing centralization of corporate decision making. In 1979 the two largest industrial corporations, Exxon and General Motors, had combined sales of $150 billion; after adjusting for inflation this was greater than the combined sales of the 200,000 manufacturing businesses operating around 1900. Not only have corporations become larger, but they control an increasing share of industrial activity. In 1947 the 200 largest industrial corporations controlled about 45 percent of all industrial assets; today their share is about 66 percent. The share held by the top 200 today exceeds the share held by the top 1,000 in 1950. Within large industrial subsectors, concentration is growing even more rapidly. For example, between 1950 and 1978 the top fifty food firms' share of all food manufacturers' assets rose from 36 to 64 percent.[3] At this rate, these large conglomerates will control virtually all food manufacturing assets by the year 2000.

The growing importance of the largest corporations is all the more impressive because it is occurring within an ever expanding universe wherein many established industries continue to grow and many entirely new industries are born each decade. These statistics suggest the central role that a relatively few corporations play in running our economy, but their importance does not derive solely from their huge and growing share of overall economic activity. Another feature of these enterprises is their tendency to operate in many separate markets, many of which are highly concentrated and dominated by these largest corporations. This is the source of much of the economic power of the large American corporation, the power of a deep pocket filled with monopoly profits.

This private power can be used for good or ill, and how it is used affects all of us. It is hardly surprising, therefore, that in a democratic society a system of social controls has evolved to place restraints on private economic power.

Concern with these matters has given birth to various types of social control of corporate enterprise. The Sherman Antitrust Act of 1890 was this nation's first effort (at the national level) to adopt a means of social control designed to use competitive market forces as the means of disciplining private enterprises. Writing in 1911,

Supreme Court Justice John M. Harlan characterized the mood that gave birth to the Sherman Act:

> All who recall the condition of the country in 1890 will remember that there was everywhere, among the people generally, a deep feeling of unrest. The nation had been rid of human slavery—fortunately, as all now feel—but the conviction was universal that the country was in real danger from another kind of slavery sought to be fastened on the American people; namely, the slavery that would result from aggregations of capital in the hands of a few individuals and corporations controlling, for their own profit and advantage exclusively, the entire business of the country, including the production and sale of the necessities of life.[4]

Today, many persons believe the antitrust approach begun in 1890 has been made obsolete by changes in industrial organization and improved economic wisdom about our system. Alan Greenspan, chairman of the Council of Economic Advisors under President Nixon, put it this way: "The Sherman Act may be understandable when viewed as a projection of 19th Century fear and economic ignorance. But it is utter nonsense in the context of today's economic knowledge."[5]

Much of the new economic wisdom originates in the teachings and preachings of "Chicago School" economists. These laissez-faire scholars argue that competition is more intense today than in 1890, which may explain why Milton Friedman and others frequently espouse social policies reminiscent of nineteenth-century economic Darwinism.

However, the world of Adam Smith has not been reborn. The great weight of empirical evidence supports the view that today market power is the rule, not the exception, in most important industries. Therefore, while an antitrust public policy may be ineffective and otherwise imperfect, it cannot be dismissed on grounds that excessive concentrations of economic power no longer exist to impose a heavy burden on our economy.

THE COSTS OF MARKET POWER

Various estimates have been made of the costs imposed on consumers by the holders of market power. Numerous econometric

studies have demonstrated a positive relationship between market concentration and the level of profits. But monopoly profits generally
understate the full costs of monopoly power. Sometimes firms have
higher costs because the absence of competition permits them to lead
the quiet life whose handmaiden is inflated costs.[6] Other firms pursue
strategies in which higher prices can only be achieved through higher
costs. For these reasons, the costs of market power are only partially
reflected by inflated profits. Therefore, studies that examine relationships between market power and price levels are preferable to those
that examine relationships between market power and profits.

Such price studies have now been made in several industries.[7] My
initial findings in a study examining prices of grocery product
manufacturers show that in many products the leading brand com-
mands a large price premium over lesser brands and private labels.
These differences in prices appear to be far greater than the differences
in profits earned on these brands, suggesting that those able to com-
mand the high prices also have higher costs as a result of extensive
advertising, product proliferation, or other factors inflating manufacturing and distribution costs.

Parker and Connor's study of food manufacturing found that
consumers pay an enormous tribute to the holders of market power.
Using alternative procedures, Parker and Connor estimate monopoly
overcharges at 7.3 percent of sales, or $12.5 billion in 1975.[8] Some
economists express disbelief in these findings, simply asserting that
this estimate is absurdly high. My own preliminary analysis confirms
that these estimates are realistic.

By manipulating consumer demand through advertising, many
grocery product firms have succeeded in escalating prices over time.
The dynamics of this process are illustrated by events in the beer industry, which historically was quite decentralized and offered consumers a considerable range of choice.

Following Philip Morris's acquisition of Miller Brewing Company
in 1970, Miller's advertising and promotion outlays were accelerated.
In 1972 Philip Morris–Miller bought the Lite beer brand. Subsequent
promotion is a classic example of advertising-created product differen-
tiation, allowing a product that costs less to make to be sold at a
premium price. Philip Morris–Miller followed up its Lite campaign
with an enormous advertising blitz of its recently acquired Lowenbrau
brand, attempting to position it as a major factor in the superpremium
market segment.

Other brewers responded to these moves by accelerating promotion of their own premium and superpremium brands of beer. The result has been skyrocketing promotional outlays, especially for television advertising, where the top five brewers' expenditures rose from $45 million in 1972 to $232 million in 1979, an increase of 415 percent.

The Lite story is only a play within a larger play, the consistent theme of which is to persuade consumers to switch to premium and superpremium beer brands. I estimate that the leading brewers' success in increasing the share of premium and superpremium beers from about 30 percent of beer sales in 1970 to 70 percent in 1980 cost beer drinkers about $500 million in 1980. Nor have consumer benefits been commensurate with the higher prices paid. There is no evidence that consumers can detect real taste differences among beers in blind tests. As Scherer says, "American consumers pay their premium price mainly for the label rather than for the quality of the contents."[9]

Monopoly overcharges in food are only part of the total monopoly overcharge bill in our economy. Scherer estimated that in the late 1960s the total costs of market power were about 9.2 percent of the gross national product (GNP).[10] Applied to the 1979 GNP, this would amount to a staggering $210 billion. Clearly, the market power problem has not withered since the Sherman Act was enacted. On the contrary, the problem has grown, in my judgment, and will continue to grow unless steps are taken to cope with it.

The preceding estimates of the magnitude of the problem may well understate its full costs. An increasing number of economists and public policy officials have come to believe that the ubiquitousness of market power creates serious problems in running the American economy as well as all other capitalistic market economies at full employment without excessive inflation.

A brief summary of the argument follows.[11] The crux of the matter is that market power creates an inflationary bias in our economy. Orthodox economic theory asserts that the price level rises and falls only as we change aggregate demand. The only cause of inflation, according to this theory, is too few goods being chased by too much money; this is called demand-pull inflation. If this were the only cause of inflation, it could be controlled quite simply by contracting aggregate demand. A heroic assumption of this theory, however, is that prices and wages are determined by free-market forces. If this were so, there would not be such a thing as a wage-price spiral nor would prices and wages fail to fall when aggregate demand declined.

Unfortunately, the real world does not conform to this simple theory; instead, prices and wages often rise in the face of falling demand. The behavior of the steel industry during the 1950s is a classic example of so-called administered or market-power–caused inflation. Prices were raised repeatedly in the face of falling demand. The inflationary pressures caused by this perverse behavior were carefully studied by economists during the 1950s.[12]

The events of the 1950s set the stage for the policies adopted in the 1960s. The Kennedy-Johnson guideposts for noninflationary wage and price behavior called for the kind generated by competitive markets. Most importantly, they were an explicit recognition that it was impossible to achieve full employment without inflation by relying solely on free-market forces.

These guideposts were quite successful in permitting noninflationary expansion until about 1966, when overstimulation of the economy caused demand-pull inflation. However, the guideposts were moderately successful in containing inflation despite the inflationary pressures of the Vietnam War. In January 1969 consumer prices rose at an annual rate of only 4.8 percent despite an unemployment rate of only 3.3 percent; moreover, the budget had a healthy running surplus.

Subsequent events should be recalled for those with short or faulty memories. This may be a case where, in the words of Oliver Wendell Holmes, a page of history is worth a volume of logic.

Under President Nixon, the free market was given a historic modern-day opportunity to prove its ability to deal with the inflation-unemployment problem. Shortly after his inauguration, Nixon made a solemn pledge: he would bring about price stability without significantly increasing unemployment, and he would accomplish this victory without any government intervention in the marketplace. As America's number-one football fan, he laid out his "game plan" for achieving this victory. The plan was simple: retard the growth in aggregate demand by balancing the budget and curtail the money supply, and free-market forces would do the rest. As the growth in aggregate demand slowed, prices would stop rising and the inflation would be brought under control. All this would be accomplished after a few "awkward months" during which high interest rates would cause some adjustment pains; slackening demand would cause a mild slowdown in production and business profits; and unemployment would rise modestly, perhaps to just over 4 percent.

The adjustment process predicted by Nixon's game plan rested on the assumption that business would respond to slackening demand by not raising prices or, better still, by reducing prices and that labor would settle for small wage increases as inflation slowed and the demand for labor slackened "modestly." President Nixon translated into policy his faith in free-market forces by stating publicly just six days after his inauguration, and periodically thereafter, that he did not intend to interfere with particular price and wage decisions as had been done during the 1960s. Indeed, for thirty-one months the Office of the President did not interfere with price or wage decisions except for a few instances in the construction industry.

Seldom in our history has a president put an economic theory to such a persistent test, and seldom have the economic costs of error been higher. During 1969 and 1970 fiscal and monetary policies generally followed the Nixon game plan, but prices failed to follow the role assigned to them: instead of moderating, they rose.

Because prices increased in the face of declining demand, the available supply of goods could not be sold at the higher prices. As a result, the utilization of manufacturing productive capacity fell from 85 percent in the first quarter of 1969 to 73 percent in the third quarter of 1971. At the same time, unemployment rose from 3.3 percent to 6.1 percent. This excess capacity cut sharply into corporate profits. Declining profits plus a general loss of investor confidence in the president's game plan triggered the sharpest stock market decline since the Great Depression. The game plan did not lead to the end run around rising prices and high unemployment predicted by the president's economic advisors.

On August 15, 1971, the president acknowledged that the plan had failed, and he unveiled an entirely new "economic plan," a system of wage and price controls. Where did the original plan go wrong? Why did prices not respond to the declining demand as predicted? The fatal flaw was the fundamental assumption that free-market forces were sufficiently powerful to discipline key price and wage decision makers in the economy. Clearly they were not.

Many events have occurred since Nixon's great experiment with free markets. The dramatic rise in oil prices and other external shocks have created new inflationary forces. But one thing seems clear: our economic system is not sufficiently flexible to absorb such shocks without experiencing high unemployment or excessive inflation or both.

It is axiomatic that those who ignore history are destined to repeat the mistakes of the past. Like President Ford, President Carter tried once again to rely solely on restrictive monetary and fiscal policy to quell inflation. This policy deliberately and purposefully weakens our economy to purge it of inflationary forces. Unhappily, this is our only option as long as we rely on market forces alone.

This inevitably raises the question of whether to abandon, partially at least, our sole reliance on market forces by adopting some system of wage and price controls. Most economists assert with great conviction that wage and price controls are an unacceptable alternative. Why? Everyone knows, say these holders of the conventional wisdom, that price controls have never worked. This is nonsense. Merely because a majority of economists agree about a matter does not make it so. For as Alfred Marshall said, "Nothing should be so much distrusted as the majority view in economics."

The truth is that controls have worked, and even though Nixon's program was administered by unsympathetic persons,[13] phases one and two did work surprisingly well. It is well to recall that the Dow-Jones industrial average of stock prices reached its historic high in January 1973. But when President Nixon announced in that month the termination of phase two of his control program, which signaled the end of effective controls, sophisticated investors knew that the decision to rely solely on monetary and fiscal policy would result in a deep recession. Experience proved them correct. The Dow-Jones average fell from its lofty height of 1,052 in January 1973 to 558 in January 1975. Thus, while most investors and business people abhor controls in the abstract, they generally fare better under controls than during recessions.

Economists are quick to condemn controls, mainly because of fear that they will create serious distortions in the allocation of resources. Yet these are trivial compared to the enormous "distortions" that accompany contractional monetary and fiscal policy, that is, high interest rates, high unemployment, underutilization of productive capacity, and depressed profits. To expect otherwise requires a triumph of hope over experience. According to Okun's Law, as the economy departs from full employment, each 1 percent increase in unemployment results in a 3 percent decrease in the GNP. In 1980 terms, that means a 3 percent increase in unemployment would cause the GNP to decline by over $200 billion. This waste of human and economic resources vastly exceeds the economic distortions so many economists fear as by-products of controls.

These policies also greatly increase our national debt. For example, the greatest federal deficits in peacetime occurred during 1975–1976, a staggering $124 billion. This exceeded by $27 billion the entire increase in the national debt between 1945 and 1973. Likewise, talk about balancing the budget is pure nonsense. I predict the recession induced by the Carter adminstration will frustrate these efforts.

So where does this leave us? It finally comes down to this: either we have wage and price controls or high unemployment and/or excessive inflation. Although I do not always agree with John K. Galbraith, I am disposed to like his strategy of confining such controls to the price decisions of the several hundred largest corporations and to the wages of the largest labor unions. I do not believe it is necessary to control smaller businesses, except perhaps in health care, and certainly not competitive industries like farming.

The breadth of controls will depend upon the extent to which we keep competition alive. So in a sense we face the choice of more controls or more competition. The greater the area of competition, the smaller the area requiring controls.

PROCOMPETITION POLICIES

This brings us to the question, What public policies should be used to prevent further centralization of economic power and to increase competition where needed? I will discuss only two policies: more effective merger enforcement and industrial restructuring of highly concentrated industries.

Conglomerate Mergers. Merger policy is the essential first step in preventing further increases in concentration in particular markets and overall centralization of power in the economy. Merger policy has been very effective in preventing mergers between direct competitors; that is, so-called horizontal mergers. Since 1950 there has been an enormous merger enforcement effort; between 1950 and 1979 the Federal Trade Commission (FTC) and Justice Department issued about 450 merger complaints challenging over 1,500 mergers, most of which were horizontal. I am confident that these actions prevented many industries from becoming highly concentrated and permitted erosion of concentration in others.[14]

However, this enforcement effort has left virtually untouched the numerous conglomerate mergers occurring since 1950. Given the enormous growth of the economy in the postwar period, the share of the economy controlled by the few hundred largest corporations probably would have declined, not increased, in the absence of such mergers. Though there is much we do not know about the causes and effects of conglomerate mergers, we know much more today than during the great merger wave that peaked in 1968–1969. At that time, many journalists, business people, and economists said the accelerating conglomerate merger activity reflected a new era, a superior economic order led by individuals of vision and superior managerial skills.

Many economists, who never learned about conglomerate power because their graduate training focused solely on market power within particular industries, were inclined to dismiss what they did not understand. Interestingly, Joan Robinson, who did much to refine the theory of imperfect competition, says in the introduction to the latest edition of her classic work that it contributes little to understanding the modern conglomerate. "My old-fashioned comparison between monopoly and competition may still have some application to old-fashioned rings, but it cannot comprehend the great octopuses of modern industry."[15]

A growing body of empirical work demonstrates that many of the sanguine interpreters of the great merger wave of the 1960s were merely rationalizing events rather than explaining their causes. Dennis C. Mueller of Cornell University recently made a most comprehensive and insightful review of the voluminous research in this area.[16] He concluded that considerations other than efficiency motivated most large conglomerate mergers. But a question still remains: Even if conglomerate mergers generally do not improve efficiency, are there any reasons for placing restraints on such mergers? Economics can only provide a partial answer. Noneconomic considerations are probably more important here, just as they always have been in formulating our antitrust laws. Ultimately, the people must decide what kind of economic system they want. This involves social and political considerations as well as purely economic ones.

Economists differ in answering this question. If one starts with the proposition that it is our national policy to promote a system of competitive, decentralized capitalism, two propositions follow. First, there is no persuasive evidence that large conglomerate acquisitions promote this objective. Second, there is evidence that large conglomerate mergers can have various adverse effects.[17] The ultimate cumulative effect of numerous large mergers may be to create an economy dominated by conglomerate enterprises unresponsive to competitive forces.

Fortune magazine summed up one such danger, that resulting from extensive reciprocal trading among large conglomerates; that is, "trade relations between the giant conglomerates tend to close a business circle, left out are the firms with narrow product lines; as patterns of trade and trading partners emerge between particular groups of companies, entry by newcomers becomes more difficult." Indeed, *Fortune* concluded that "the United States economy might end up completely dominated by conglomerates happily trading with each other in a new kind of cartel system."[18] But reciprocal trading is only a symptom of the larger problem of conglomerate interdependence and competitive forbearance in an economy in which most commerce is controlled by a few huge corporations.

The *Wall Street Journal* editorialized at the peak of the great conglomerate merger wave of the late 1960s that:

> Unchecked expansion of conglomerates would eventually reduce competition and impair the efficiency of our approximation of a free market economy. When ties among large corporations get too widespread and too involved, it seems to us they will impede the free movement of prices and capital even if the merged corporations are not in the same field. Certainly, the consolidation of various corporations into conglomerates could invite a vastly increased concentration of economic power, which gives us pause on both economic and social grounds.[19]

Conglomerate mergers also impact adversely on our social institutions. Various studies, including some done by members of the Business School of the University of Wisconsin, have found that mergers, especially conglomerate ones, often impact adversely on communities in a variety of ways. These include a reduction in the use of legal, financial, accounting, and advertising services in the acquired firm's community and a decline in participation in community affairs by top management.[20]

Similarly, ever-increasing centralization of economic power is inconsistent with our political institutions. William O. Douglas articulated the view that such power is contrary to proper functioning of democratic institutions. As he put it, "Industrial power should be decentralized so that the fortunes of the people will not be dependent on the whim or caprice, the political prejudices, the emotional stability of a few self-appointed men. The fact that they are not vicious men but respectable men is irrelevant.''

Nor can these concerns be dismissed by asserting that they are bogeymen created by critics of capitalism, as implied in a lead article in *Fortune* attacking Senator Ted Kennedy's conglomerate merger bill.[21] Significantly, in the same issue an article examining ''The New Divisions of U.S. Politics'' revealed that 51 percent of Americans with incomes of $25,000 or more believed that ''big business is becoming a threat to the American way of life.''[22] The fact that a majority of the most fortunate beneficiaries of American capitalism hold this view should give pause to those who prefer to believe that no real public concern exists for the issue of conglomerate-created centralization of economic power.

Many thoughtful business people are becoming concerned with the swelling wave of conglomerate mergers. A longtime student of our system, A.C. Hoffman, retired vice-president of Kraft, Inc., observed, ''At the present rate at which American industry is being merged and consolidated, we will indeed reach that ultimate stage of monopoly capitalism which Marx predicted—and about 100 years ahead of schedule.''[23]

There was a time when it appeared that existing law was adequate to deal with conglomerate mergers. In 1969 Richard McLaren, the newly appointed head of the Antitrust Division, announced that he would challenge all large conglomerate mergers unless he received an adverse decision from the Supreme Court.[24]

McLaren did more than talk. He challenged a series of large conglomerate mergers during 1969–1970. The most famous of these were three separate acquisitions by ITT, itself a large conglomerate. After prosecuting these cases aggressively for two years and after one had reached the Supreme Court, the Justice Department in a surprise move settled all three cases. The main effect of this action was to prevent the Supreme Court, headed by Chief Justice Earl Warren, from rendering a decision in any of these crucial cases.

Subsequent events proved that McLaren's efforts foundered, as Henry C. Simons might have said, on ''the orderly process of democratic corruption.'' ITT's extensive lobbying efforts at all levels of government are well documented.[25] But we are indebted to the release of the famous White House tapes for an insight as to President Nixon's views of and involvement in the ITT cases. The president objected strenuously when McLaren, then assistant attorney general, took action against ITT. The following are excerpts from a telephone conversation between the president and Deputy Attorney General Richard Kleindienst, which took place on April 19, 1971, from 3:04 to 3:09 P.M. The conversation occurred on the eve of the Department of Justice's filing of its brief before the Supreme Court, appealing a district court's decision in the *U.S.* v. *ITT-Grinnell* merger case.

Kleindienst: Hi, Mr. President.

President: Hi, Dick, how are you?

Kleindienst: Good, how are you, sir?

President: Fine, fine. I'm going to talk to John [Mitchell] tomorrow about my general attitude on antitrust,

Kleindienst: Yes, sir.

President: and in the meantime, I know that he has left with you, uh, the IT&T thing because apparently he says he had something to do with them once.*

Kleindienst: (Laughs) Yeah. Yeah.

President: Well, I have, I have nothing to do with them, and I want something clearly understood, and, if it is not understood, McLaren's ass is to be out within one hour. The IT&T thing—stay the hell out of it. Is that clear? That's an order.

Kleindienst: Well, you mean the order is to. . . .

President: The order is to leave the God-damned thing alone. Now, I've said this, Dick, a number of times, and you fellows apparently don't get the me . . ., the message over there. I do not want McLaren to run around prosecuting people, raising hell about conglomerates, stirring things up at this point. Now you keep him the hell out of that. Is that clear?

Kleindienst: Well, Mr. President. . . .

President: Or either he resigns. I'd rather have him out anyway. I don't like the son-of-a-bitch.

Kleindienst: The, the question then is. . . .

President: The question is, I know, that the Jurisdiction . . . I know all the legal things, Dick, you don't have to spell out the legal. . . .

Kleindienst: (Unintelligible) the appeal filed.

President: That's right.

Kleindienst: That brief has to be filed tomorrow.†

President: That's right. Don't file the brief.

---

* Because Attorney General John Mitchell had represented ITT, he was required to disqualify himself in the ITT Cases and delegate his responsibilities to Richard Kleindienst, deputy attorney general.

† This is a reference to the appeal brief to the Supreme Court in the ITT-Grinnell case.

Kleindienst:	Your order is not to file a brief?
President:	Your . . . my order is to drop the God-damn thing. Is that clear?
Kleindienst:	(Laughs) Yeah, I understand that.
President:	Okay.
Kleindienst:	(Unintelligible)
	(President hangs up.)

The Nixon-Kleindienst telephone conversation occurred during a meeting at which the president was talking about antitrust policy with his Budget Bureau Director George Schultz and domestic advisor John Ehrlichman. Not too surprisingly, Schultz, on leave from the University of Chicago, was reassuring the president that conglomerate mergers posed no competitive problem. The president agreed, expressing the view that antitrust policy may have been a good thing for the country for fifty years, but, as he saw it, "It's not a good thing for the country today." He then walked up to the brink of acknowledging that his concern with the ITT cases reflected the pressure ITT's Chairman Harold Geneen had been putting on the administration. But then he protested, one suspects too loudly, that Geneen had not really influenced his thinking. The president commented that the Justice Department "had raised holy hell with the people we, uh, uh . . . well, Geneen, hell, he's no contributor. He's nothing to us. I don't care about him. So you can . . . I've only met him once, twice . . . uh, we've, I'm just, uh . . .I can't understand what the trouble is." Nixon then continued, "It's McLaren, isn't it?" To which Ehrlichman responded, "McLaren has a very strong sense of mission here."

Ehrlichman's defense of McLaren obviously enraged Nixon.

President:	Good . . . Jesus, he's . . . get him out. In one hour.
Ehrlichman:	He's got a . . .
President:	One hour.
Ehrlichman:	very strong . . .
President:	And he's not going to be a judge either. He is out of the God-damn government. You know, just like that regional office man in, in, San Francisco. I put an order in to Haldeman today that he be fired today.
Ehrlichman:	Yeah.

The rest of the story is well known. At the time of the Nixon-

Ehrlichman conversation, McLaren was being considered for appoint-
ment to the federal bench. He was ultimately persuaded to settle the
ITT cases, after which he was appointed a federal judge in the Northern District of Illinois.

Over a decade has passed since McLaren failed in his effort to
clarify the legal status of conglomerate mergers under existing law. In
the meantime, conglomerate merger activity has continued virtually
untouched. At this point, only the direct legislative approach is adequate to the task. One example of such an approach is the bill cospon-
sored by senators Ted Kennedy and Howard Metzenbaum. Such
legislation would prohibit all very large mergers unless their proponents could prove the mergers were procompetitive or otherwise
served the public interest.

Industrial Reorganization of Concentrated Industries. Excessive market concentration pervades much of the American economy.
Under existing law the antitrust agencies cannot effectively challenge
entrenched monopolists. In 1969 the Justice Department charged the
International Business Machines Corporation (IBM) as a monopolist in
violation of the Sherman Act. After more than eleven years of bitter
legal battles, it appears that the government is about to succumb and
settle the case without benefit of a court decision. Nor has the Justice
Department fared any better in its monopoly case against the
American Telephone and Telegraph Company (AT & T). The FTC
concedes that its 1973 monopoly case against leading petroleum companies "has ground to a halt." And its big "shared-monopoly" case
against leading cereal companies is bogged down in legal technicali-
ties. In 1982 the Department of Justice recommended dismissal of the
IBM case. This dismissal is (spring 1982) being challenged in federal
court by a number of private parties. In 1982 the Department of
Justice recommended that the AT & T case be settled with a consent
decree. A federal court is (spring 1982) holding hearings on the proposed settlement. In January 1982 the Federal Trade Commission
dismissed its shared monopoly case against the three leading cereal
companies.

Under existing law the antitrust agencies are outgunned and out-
numbered in these big cases, each of which becomes a legal Vietnam.
After years of indecisive legal battles, the government settles for far
less than total victory. This effectively leaves the chief bastions of
power essentially immune from antitrust challenge. If we are serious

about increasing competition in problem industries, new approaches are needed.

Remedying this situation requires a new mandate from the Congress indicating support for efforts to improve competition in the economy and a new statute that provides effective and expeditious mechanisms for accomplishing this goal.

New legislation along the lines of the late Senator Philip Hart's Industrial Reorganization Act is required. The key to this approach is a rebuttable presumption that a corporation is violating the law if certain structural and/or performance criteria are met. This approach has the virtue of shifting much of the burden of proof to the defendant.

Finally, any reform aimed at dismantling monopolies must include initiatives directed at the role played by modern advertising in the achievement and maintenance of market power. Empirical studies have shown that large-scale advertising, especially for products best promoted by television, is the major source of growing market concentration.[26] While advocates of reform can always expect a hostile reception by special interest groups, nowhere is this more true than in advertising. Attempts by special interest groups to dismantle the FTC stem largely from its investigation of advertising directed at children.

But this makes it all the more important that academicians participate in efforts to develop new policy initiatives in the area of advertising. There is no ready-made panacea for dealing with the problem. Any across-the-board approach is likely to be too simple to be effective. But the stakes are high. In 1980 over $50 billion was spent on advertising and promotional efforts, the main effect of which was to persuade rather than inform. Some economists rationalize these huge expenditures on grounds that we can afford a good deal of waste in our affluent economy. I suspect this view will be challenged as we become increasingly concerned with private as well as public actions that wastefully consume human and natural resources.

CONCLUSIONS

After all is said and done, antitrust policy will not cure all the problems mentioned, but this is not sufficient grounds for abandoning this policy. I am receptive to alternatives. But after considering those being offered today, I am still very impressed with the many virtues of a competitive market-oriented economy. While sympathetic to much of Professor Galbraith's view of the world, I do not agree that antitrust policy can only be a "charade."[27] The trouble with Galbraith is that he does not appreciate or understand the many successes of antitrust policy in maintaining effectively competitive markets. I readily forgive him these errors, although I have brought them to his attention from time to time. The main point is that even if we concede Galbraith's assertion that many markets perform poorly, a powerful case remains for expanding the areas where competition works sufficiently well to make public intervention unnecessary. Reducing the areas requiring direct government intervention is one of the greatest virtues of procompetition policies. While all may not agree that the government that governs least is best, all will agree, I am sure, that no government should govern unnecessarily.

NOTES

1. Harold C. Livesay, *American Made,* (Boston: Little, Brown, 1979).
2. H. Sampson, *The Sovereign State of ITT* (New York: Stein and Day, 1973), p. 125.
3. J. M. Connor, *The U.S. Food and Tobacco Manufacturing Industries,* Agricultural Economics Report 451, ESCS, USDA, March 1980, p. 10.
4. *Standard Oil Co. of New Jersey* v. *United States,* 221 U.S. 83(1911).
5. Alan Greenspan, "Antitrust," in Ayn Rand, *Capitalism: The Unknown Ideal* (New York: New American Library, 1967), p. 56.
6. H. Leibenstein, "Allocative Efficiency v. X-Efficiency," *American Economic Review* (June 1966):37.
7. Weiss summarizes studies in banking and petroleum distribution in food retailing. See Leonard W. Weiss, "The Structure-Conduct-Performance Paradigm and Antitrust," *The Pennsylvania Law Review* 123(1972): 1107–15. Another study on food retailing is L. Hall, A. Schmitz, and J. Cothern, "Beef Marketing Margins and Concentration," *Economica* (Aug. 1979):295–300.
8. R. C. Parker and J. M. Connor, "Estimates of Consumer Loss to Monopoly in the U.S. Food Manufacturing Industries," *American Journal of Agricultural Economics* (Nov. 1979):631.
9. F. M. Scherer, "The Posnerian Harvest: Separating the Wheat from Chaff," *Yale Law Review* (Apr. 1977):997–98.
10. F. M. Scherer, *Industrial Market Structure and Economic Performance* (Chicago: Rand McNally 1971), pp. 408–9.
11. For my views on the subject, see W. F. Mueller, "Industrial Concentration: An Important Inflationary Force," in H. J. Goldschmid et al., *Industrial Concentration: The New Learning* (New York: Little, Brown, 1974), pp. 280–306.

12. See especially O. Eckstein and G. Fromm, *Steel and the Post-War Infla-tion,* Joint Economic Committee Study Paper no. 2, 86th Congress, 1st Session, November 6, 1959.

13. C. Jackson Grayson, Jr., with Louis Neeb, *Confessions of a Price Con-troller* (Homewood: Dow Jones–Irwin, 1974).

14. W. F. Mueller, *The Celler-Kefauver Act: The First 25 Years,* a study prepared for the use of the Subcommittee on Monopolies and Commer-cial Law of the Committee on the Judiciary, House of Representatives, 96th Congress, 1st Session, November 7, 1969.

15. Joan Robinson, *The Economics of Imperfect Competition*, 2nd ed. (New York: St. Martin, 1969), p. xi.

16. Dennis C. Mueller, "The Effects of Conglomerate Mergers," *Journal of Banking and Finance* 1(1977):315.

17. W. F. Mueller, "Conglomerates: A Non-Industry," in W. Adams, ed., *The Structure of American Industry* (New York: Macmillan, 1977), pp. 441–81.

18. *Fortune,* June 1965, p. 194.

19. *Wall Street Journal,* March 26, 1969, p. 20.

20. Jon G. Udell, "Social and Economic Consequences of Merger Movement in Wisconsin," Bureau of Business Research and Services, University of Wisconsin, Madison, May 1969.

21. "Bigness Becomes the Target of the Trustbusters," *Fortune,* March 26, 1979, p. 34.

22. Ibid., p. 91.

23. A. C. Hoffman, "Trends in the Food Industries and Their Relationship to Agriculture. In Leon Garoian, ed., *Economics of Conglomerate Growth,* Agricultural Research Foundation, Oregon State University, Corvallis, November 1969, p. 57.

24. W. F. Mueller, "The ITT Settlement: A Deal with Justice?" *Industrial Organization Review* 1(1973):68–69.

25. Ibid.

26. W. F. Mueller and R. T. Rogers, "The Role of Advertising in Changing Concentration of Manufacturing Industries," *Review of Economics and Statistics* (Feb. 1980):89–95.

27. See testimony of J. K. Galbraith and W. F. Mueller, Hearings on Plan-ning Regulation and Competition, Subcommittees of the Select Com-mittee on Small Business, U.S. Senate, 90th Congress, 1st Session, June 29, 1967, pp. 1–11, 17–27.

5

Markets, Agriculture, and Inflation

POPULAR perceptions of this topic are not reassuring. Free markets are out of fashion. Agriculture is viewed as an environmental hazard and, like the response to rock music, inflation is the uninhibited private behavior of people. We have corps of well-paid experts who specialize in market failures; harmful effects of agriculture as it poisons the soil, depletes cropland, and contaminates our water and food; and inflation as the inevitable consequence of private greed and the greed of the Organization of Petroleum-Exporting Countries (OPEC). Virtually every reform of the economy is promoted as a correction for what is deemed to be a market failure. The Ralph Nader experts contend that the performance of agricultural markets is incompatible with their goals of a good society. Antitrust proponents propose strange concepts of competition. Many farmers know that markets do not suffice to give them target and price-support prices. Nor do markets give labor the unemployment payments and minimum wages that organized labor wants. Many business firms want to be protected from foreign competition. There is a long-persistent argument of Professor John Galbraith's that big corporations have the monopoly power to set prices as they please and that they manipulate the market to their advantage. Consumer, health, and safety advocates want a riskless society. Environmentalists and those who speak for organized labor, farmer movements, and business enterprises that have a vested interest in government regulations are all expert witnesses for the prosecution of free markets.

Theodore W. Schultz is Charles L. Hutchinson Distinguished Professor, Department of Economics, University of Chicago. The author is indebted to Lowell Hill for his useful critical comments.

The case before the public is *Government Prices* v. *Market Prices.* The decision in this case is being made by the American people, not by economists. The electorate of this country is the jury. It is our good fortune that Congress, the executive branch, and the courts will do what the electorate decides should be done, although not all would agree that government is responsive to the electorate in view of pressure group activity. It is immodest to presume that I can instruct this august jury. As an academic economist, my commitment is to education.

My plan is to begin with the economic attributes of markets, including some aspects of international as well as domestic markets. I then turn to activities in which government has a comparative advantage and proceed to areas where it does not, that is, those areas where market prices perform better than government planners. The unrealized economic potential of the economy is next on the agenda, followed by a brief look at inflation and the market.

ECONOMIC ATTRIBUTES OF MARKETS

My instruction begins with the issue, What is the essence of a market? When two or more human agents exchange things that have some economic value, there is a market. The critical, essential part of this exchange is the agreement by these human agents on the economic value of the things that are exchanged. These are scarce and thus have some economic value. The agreed-on value is, for our purpose, the price. Markets have a long history as a means of arriving at prices. The price arrived at in an ideal market equates the marginal cost and the marginal utility of the things exchanged. The essence of a market is its price-making function. It is all too easy to lose sight of this essential activity.

There is a misguided approach that attributes various activities to markets that are standard production activities, performed not by markets, but generally by firms classified as being in the market sector. This approach tends to conceal the price-making function of markets. Agricultural markets, for example, do not produce transportation and storage nor do they process farm products into food. Since there is a demand and a supply of each of these producer services, there is a market that determines the economic value of each, that is, the price of each of these services. A logical extension of this misguided approach to markets would be to treat all agricultural production as marketing.

By way of clarification, I have presented elsewhere two polarized models, neither of which comes close to reality.[1] They nevertheless call attention to the prevailing reality that lies between the two. The first presumes a country in which all production and consumption activities are performed by wholly self-sufficient farms and farm households. There are no markets and no explicit prices. Each self-sufficient farm family equates the costs of what it produces with the utility the family derives from its own production. The second model presumes a country in which all production is nationalized and all products are deemed to be "public goods" distributed free of charge to consumers. Here too there are no markets and no explicit prices. Between these highly simplified polarized models are the intricacies of market and government prices. The economics of market prices and political prices are very different. A free-market price is a consequence of matching offers and bids; the price that is agreed on clears the market. The supply-offer price tends toward the price that is equal to the marginal costs of production, and the demand-bid price tends toward the marginal utility that consumers derive from the purchase. A politically determined price is a consequence of actions taken by the government; it benefits the interest group that has sufficient political influence to obtain this benefit. The cost is (as a rule) so widely diffused that those who bear it have less political influence than those who benefit.

There is an East-West Conference story to the effect that when every country of the world has established a centrally controlled economy, it will be necessary to force one country to revert to free-market prices so that the rest will be able to observe what the real economic values are!

Since human agents arrive at prices by various means and at many different locations, some elaboration of what occurs may be helpful. When a farmer sells grain or livestock to another farmer, it is a market transaction at an agreed price. There is also an implicit price when neighbors exchange work or gifts are exchanged, as field studies by anthropologists of so-called primitive communities show. Each of these price-making activities is location specific, be it a neighborhood or a community. The demand and supply that make the price may be local, national, or international. The pricing may be done on a specific trading floor or at many locations connected by a national or international network. The physical entities involved in market transactions include commodities, goods, equipment, structures, land, and all manner of other natural resources. There are corresponding transactions for services, for example, insurance, credit, and the leased services of a wide array of different types of property, from computers to land. Every farmer knows that to rent farmland is to engage in an ongoing market for the services of land. The contracts between organized labor and employers pertain to the services of labor. Universities commit themselves to faculty tenure.

An important attribute of many market transactions is that they entail future price commitments. The longer the future specified in these transactions, the larger the risk and uncertainty. Measurement of what is being dealt in is a critical factor in limiting the extent of the market. As measurement becomes more ambiguous, the market becomes more restricted because risk and uncertainty increase. The specifications of a bushel of wheat are sufficiently precise and enforceable to make it possible to have not only a national but an international market for wheat, including both spot and future transactions; but they are less so in the case of potatoes, other vegetables, or fresh fruits.

INTERNATIONAL ASPECTS

My instruction to the electorate would also stress the point that foreign exchange markets make it abundantly clear that the international price of the dollar is not fixed by the U.S. government. International commodity agreements that specify future prices fail because the future supply and demand tend to prevail and the incentive to use the market prices is stronger than the agreement. In every dynamic, modernizing economy, changes are constantly occurring. There are also shocks, for instance, a run of poor crops. Then too, there are surprises such as the embargo of grain sales to the Union of Soviet Socialist Republics (USSR). When the European Community (EC), Japan, and other countries stabilize their internal grain prices, the effect of such stabilization is to transfer price instability to the remaining world market for grains. Professor D. Gale Johnson has established this interaction as a valid economic proposition.[2] It is still fair game, however, for one country to export its price instability to others. The time has come to challenge and eliminate that game. Johnson's economic proposition is also applicable when it comes to stabilizing particular internal agricultural commodity prices. If the prices of half our agricultural products were stabilized, it would add to the instability of the other half as shocks and surprises occurred.

There is much confusion about what the government can do better than the market and, in turn, what the market can do better than the government. The confusion is enhanced by zealous advocates of government intervention. Part of my instruction to the electorate is to help clarify the state of the evidence.

GOVERNMENT'S COMPARATIVE ADVANTAGES

When writing the Constitution, our founders, in their wisdom, were explicit that national defense, civil order, and the mediation of internal conflicts are functions of government. Experience over time, however, has made it evident that there are additional functions that govenment can do better than the private sector. With some qualifications, the government has a comparative advantage in doing the following.

It has a marked advantage in producing and reporting agricultural statistics. Statistics are an important source of information in determining prices. U.S. Department of Agriculture (USDA) statistics are not confined to the United States. They are in many respects more reliable than most United Nations (UN) statistics and those of many other countries; however, there are omissions. For example, although over half the income of U.S. farm families comes from off-farm sources, economic statistics pertaining to the sources of this off-farm income are lacking.

The USDA continues to find it convenient to mislabel some important statistics. For example, all the additional costs incurred in producing food after farmers sell their product and before consumers buy it at retail are erroneously labeled marketing spreads, marketing margins, and marketing costs. Representatives of agriculture have long been pleased by this labeling because it supports their political belief that greedy middlemen account for these "marketing margins." There is also an increasing tendency to marshall statistics in support of particular USDA programs, for instance, statistics designed to make the case for further expansion of the food stamp program. In general, statistics produced by the long-established departments of the federal government are more reliable than those put out by the Department of Energy and the many other new regulatory agencies. Beware of relying on the latter.

Measurable specifications and the enforcement of the specified measurements are also exceedingly important in pricing commodities that are bought and sold. The government has a strong comparative advantage in this domain. Advances in the technology of measurement, along with enforcement, have contributed much to increases in the extent of the market and to the resulting division of labor. The advances pertaining to weights and measures applicable to agricultural markets substantially improve the price-making process.

Inspection of products, especially food, is also done predominantly by government. The inspection of meat has a long history, although from time to time its dependability falters. The inspection of fruits, vegetables, and milk is often used to restrict the market in favor of particular producers. The inspection of imported fruits and vegetables has been much misused as a means of curtailing such imports.

The government is the primary authority in determining the property rights of buyers and sellers when things are exchanged.

The economic value of agricultural research raises a special and difficult pricing problem. The writers of the Constitution could not have anticipated this problem. The large organized research sector is a recent development. We have learned a good deal about the economics of agricultural research, which contributes much to the increases in agricultural productivity. The general rates of return on the expenditures are decidedly favorable. These rates of return tell us that it is a worthwhile activity; they also give us the implicit price of this research but do not tell us who should pay for it and how it should be organized. Consider the experiment stations, laboratories, and other university research related to agriculture. Universities do not sell their product (they make their findings available to the public) nor do they provide the funds to cover the costs of doing this research. The question of who benefits and who bears the costs requires some elaboration. There is, however, another factor. In the United States, about 25 percent of all expenditures on agricultural research is accounted for by industry. Industrial firms understandably restrict their agricultural research to projects from which they expect to derive a profit. The economics is simple and straightforward. It could be argued that the same economic logic shows that farmers should pay for the research from which they profit, just as industrial firms do.

The first difficulty in applying this logic is that, in the long run under competition, reductions in the real costs of producing agricultural products, which are results of agricultural research, are transferred in large measure to consumers. Farmers who first adopt a new high-yielding variety benefit; but when most farmers have adopted such a variety, the benefits shift to consumers. Even if farmers were the beneficiaries, it is beyond the capacity of the individual farmer to do the required research. Nor are farmers collectively able to organize and finance national agricultural research. Although most of the benefits from agricultural research accrue to consumers over time, it is not feasible for them to organize and finance national agricultural research enterprises. The only meaningful approach to modern organized agricultural research is to conceptualize most of its contributions as public goods. As such, they must be paid for on public account, which does not exclude private gifts used to produce public goods. There is a serious unresolved organizational quandary in supporting basic science research with public funds. Most of such research is done by universities. The allocation of these funds and the regulations that follow in their wake are seriously impairing the ongoing research of scientists. The institutions serving agricultural research have a longer history and are in better repair than those doing basic research in the sciences. Nevertheless, there are unsolved problems, of which perhaps the most serious is the tendency to overorganize agricultural research.[3]

Finally, there is the unstable behavior of the overall level of prices. It is strictly the responsibility of the federal government to keep the U.S. economy from surging into an inflation or falling into a depression. In terms of avoiding inflation, the government has performed badly indeed; I shall return to this problem later.

ADVANTAGES OF MARKET PRICES

The price-making activity of markets, despite all the talk about market failures, is not obsolete. Although it is obvious that there are many regulations and government interventions that distort market prices, markets continue to survive; they continue to perform most of the essential price-making functions that the economy requires. That markets should continue to be as robust as they are under the burden of the constraints placed upon them should tell us a good deal about how essential markets are in our democratic society. In my instruction to the American electorate, I suggest that serious consideration be given to the following points.

No government that has abolished markets has been successful in modernizing agriculture. The inefficiency of agricultural resource allocation in all centrally controlled economies is no longer in doubt. The USSR, with all its farm machinery, fertilizer, and other large investments in agriculture continues to be incapable of developing a modern efficient agricultural sector. From discussions in the USSR with managers of collective farms, I know they are intelligent and capable human beings. They are not to blame for the poor performance of Soviet agriculture. Orders from Moscow are poor substitutes for market prices.

In South Asia where, under colonial rule, food grains were frequently procured from farmers by force to cope with poor crops caused by bad monsoons, some governments continue to procure food grains at below market prices to provide cheap rice and wheat for fair food shops, mainly for the benefit of urban consumers.[4] The effect of such procurement is to distort the incentives of farmers and, in so doing, reduce their economic possibility to modernize agriculture. The production of rice in India, for example, has been seriously thwarted by such procurement of that commodity from farmers.

Some years ago the government of India abolished food grain markets by assuming direct control of distribution of the product. The result was disorganization verging on chaos, and the government gave up its noble experiment.

The governments of the EC are vastly overpricing major agricultural products within these countries. It is obvious to any economist that this is a costly and wasteful policy; there is a growing recognition in these countries that it is not viable. Free trade at going international prices would be a boon for consumers in the EC.

At the other extreme, many low-income countries, despite their urgent requirements for more agricultural production, are underpricing their agricultural products. In most of these countries, free trade and internal prices at the prevailing international rates would be a boon for the modernization of their agriculture.

Some low-income countries have in effect nationalized the pricing of fertilizer by controlling imports, production, and distribution of fertilizer. The inefficiency and waste of these government endeavors are well documented.

It is useful to ponder the current pronouncements in favor of freezing prices (including wages, dividends, interest, and profits) to cope with inflation. What is striking is that farm product prices are deemed to be an exception. This implies that at least something has been learned about the notable failure of past price freezes. As yet, however, many of the American electorate have not learned that inflation cannot be controlled by this action.

My final point calls attention to the interplay between international markets and import or export embargoes. The U.S. embargo on oil from Iran diverts the Iranian oil that would have come to the United States to other importing countries, and the United States buys more of its imported oil from the other oil exporters. As a consequence, the U.S. embargo has little or no effect on the overall market for Iranian oil exports. Correspondingly, the U.S. embargo on grain sales to the USSR causes the international market to reshuffle world exports and imports of these commodities.[5] It is doubtful that total U.S. exports and Soviet imports of grain will differ substantially from what had been expected before the embargo was mandated.

UNREALIZED ECONOMIC POTENTIAL

The U.S. economy is in serious disarray. The electorate is confused, not knowing what has gone wrong. For want of an economic perspective, we have distorted the economy and its potential contributions are being lost. For want of prices that are consistent with real economic values, wrong allocative decisions have become the order of the day. For want of undistorted incentives, the productivity of the economy declines.

We have a highly skilled labor force, and it is large relative to the population. We have an ample supply of competent farm and nonfarm entrepreneurs who do not shy away from risk, provided there are prospective profits. We have an abundance of many of the required natural resources. Our basic science and agricultural research are the best in the world. Our stock of useful knowledge is very large and is increasing despite the economic disarray. This knowledge is an important potential source of additional productivity. Although we are highly favored by the quantity and quality of our resources, our capacity to take advantage of them has diminished. The reason for this decline in capacity is quite obvious. We have lost sight of the requirements for a dynamic economy that is capable of coping with changes and new opportunities. The demand for and supply of most products and services are constantly changing. In a dynamic economy, disequilibriums are inevitable. They cannot be eliminated by law or public policy and certainly not by rhetoric. These disequilibriums are consequences of changes that occur over time. When they are a consequence of modernization, they entail new opportunities. In a decentralized market economy, farmers, business people, laborers, students, and consumers perceive and evaluate these opportunities and decide whether it is worthwhile to pursue them. These opportunities and the differences among them are the mainspring that propels a dynamic economy.[6] Economic shocks and surprises must also be taken in stride. There is no escape from risks and uncertainty. To have a viable, efficient, dynamic economy, there must be prices that do not distort real economic values. Currently, however, many prices are badly distorted. The leaders of various movements that are antagonistic to market and private enterprises find it all too convenient to attribute these distortions to market failures, whereas most are caused by the types of economic policy that they advocate. The critical price distortions are in large part consequences of government failures and only in small part the result of imperfections in markets per se. U.S. economic policy has become a victim of the siren songs of the proponents of a riskless society and of overzealous environmentalists. We have let the anti-science movement politicize public funding of science research.[7] The government has issued literally thousands upon thousands of regulations which, when they are enforced, entail all manner of costs, while the benefits are as a rule vague and highly controversial.[8] These regulations impose additional risks and uncertainty on the private parts of the economy. The most serious consequence of many of these regulations is that they distort prices and incentives throughout the economy.

I have devoted a book to a set of essays by competent, experienced international agricultural authorities on the distortions of agricultural incentives.[9] These distortions take a large economic toll in both low- and high-income countries, but the adverse economic consequences are in no instance, including the case of rice in India, as appalling as the consequences of distortions of energy prices in the United States. Beginning with the Emergency Petroleum Allocation Act (in 1973) the U.S. government enacted nine additional acts pertaining to energy by 1980. These laws and the regulations they mandate make a rational economic solution of the U.S. energy problem impossible. Three major studies agree on the reasons for this failure. In a critical interpretation of these studies, Vergeler summarizes the issues succinctly.

> All agree . . . that the impediments to a rational solution
> of the energy problems are, first, the price controls on all forms
> of energy that discourage conservation; second, the pernicious
> environmental regulations; third, the concealed costs of relying
> on foreign oil; fourth, the difficult and emotional questions that
> attend the use of nuclear energy; and fifth, the federal govern-
> ment's ineffectual role in supporting new elixirs like synthetic
> fuels.[10]

The economic necessity of market prices bears repeating. Any price on which buyers and sellers freely agree, each having only a small influence on the price, is one that approximates the real economic value of the thing that is exchanged. There are also cultural and social values that may not be taken into account in market prices. How to reconcile these different values is the source of much confusion. Understandably, the electorate finds itself in a quandary on some of these issues. It may be helpful to present several simplifying propositions to reduce some aspects of this confusion. Economists are fond of saying "There is no free lunch." What is noteworthy about this phrase is that it is true for any society (country) regardless of its culture, social structure, and political organization. Free food, free housing (no rent), or free health care can conceal the economic value of these things, but it cannot eliminate the cost of producing them. The marginal cost and utility of anything that is not free must be brought into harmony or there will be waste and misuse of scarce resources.

Social and cultural values do matter. They must be properly included in economic analyses as they are in most studies pertaining to human capital. Studies of investment in education do not debase the cultural aspect of education because future cultural satisfactions that students expect to derive from this investment are a part of the return. It is also true for any other investments in human capital, for instance, undertaking investments to improve and maintain one's health. In principle, any cultural or social value that entails use of scarce resources is not free. Under these conditions it becomes necessary to solve the problems of harmonizing (equating) the marginal cost and utility of the social value. The concept of externalities is not new in economics; it goes back to Pigou and his analysis of the social costs of smoke that factories belch into the air.[11] The regulatory approach to solving this class of pollution problems is inefficient compared to charging factories for their pollution, using an explicit price. The original price would be set low; if it turned out to be too low to induce factories to reduce pollution to an acceptable level, the price would be gradually increased until experience showed that it was high enough. There is no way of forecasting the costs that will be incurred as a consequence of the regulations that are now imposed, nor is it possible to forecast the benefits that will be realized as a consequence of these regulations. It is undoubtedly true that some of the current regulations are worthwhile in terms of benefits relative to the costs they impose, but others result in too few benefits to cover their costs. Many are harmful in the sense that they actually reduce real income. There are also externalities beyond the domain of the market as well as worthwhile public goods the market cannot afford to produce. I have cited organized science and agricultural research, which contribute to the stock of knowledge that enters the public domain as valuable public goods.

INFLATION AND MARKETS

We are learning, although at a high price, that inflation is not good for the economy; but this costly lesson has as yet taught us all too little. The American electorate still fails to comprehend adequately the full adverse effects of the current inflation on investment, production, savings, and distribution of personal income. Nor does the electorate understand the causes of this high rate of inflation. There are those who attribute it to the marked increases in food prices, housing costs, and health services. Others place much of the blame on what they deem to be the inordinate rise in wages. The government has learned the least, judging from what it has failed to do to solve this inflation problem. I contend that the competent economists in government know that the oil companies and big business corporations are not causing the inflation; they also know that the greed of OPEC is not the real culprit, for they must know that Japan and West Germany, which import all their oil, have not had our high rates of inflation. Farmers, business people, laborers, and consumers have not caused this inflation. They are doing the best they can to survive, facing as they do the distortions caused by it. It would be nice if OPEC would fade away, but OPEC oil prices, costly as they are, could have been taken in stride by the U.S. economy had the government permitted rational economic prices. Rational prices would have resulted in higher energy prices than we had during the seventies, but any increase in one price relative to other prices is not the essence of inflation.

Our inflation is the handiwork of our government, and it is fair to say that the fueling of inflation by government is in large measure a consequence of policies and programs that American voters have been demanding. The majority of the electorate is ultimately responsible. It is not evident that this majority has learned its lesson pertaining to the causes of inflation. The outlook continues to be dim in regard to a rational pricing of energy. It is not encouraging in view of the rhetoric and apparent support for a quick fix of inflation by freezing all prices, wages, interests, dividends, and profits, which would only conceal it and greatly increase price distortions that are already serious. The outlook is bleak, considering the weak proposals for changes in fiscal policy that would support an appropriate monetary policy.

Private economic agents have come to expect inflation. What they can do to reduce their losses or even benefit from it varies widely, depending on the accuracy of how they perceive inflation and on economic circumstances that constrain their ability to adjust to it. When government officials state that the government is about to "stop" the inflation, these declarations of intent are no longer taken seriously by most private economic agents because of past failures of the government to deliver on what it promised to achieve. When officials assure the public that no price and wage controls will be mandated, business and labor hasten to increase their prices and wages on the assumption that price and wage controls are indeed in the making, judging from past experience.

Looking at the investment records of many farmers, beginning with the seventies, shows that what they have done is consistent with expectations that a high rate of inflation would occur. Their economic behavior implies that they have expected inflation. They have overinvested in durables by buying more equipment and expensive machinery than they would have under normal (noninflationary) expectations; more importantly, they have invested heavily in that long-life durable, farmland.[12] After allowing for the increases in their debts, many of them have increased their real net wealth as a consequence of land prices having risen at a higher rate than prices in general. I am sure that most economists have done much less well in changing their portfolios of assets than these farmers have in coping with the inflation of the seventies. The puzzle is, how did the farmers arrive at and act on the expectations of inflation that have guided their investments? People who own their homes and farmers who own land may well have a vested interest in more inflation.

CONCLUSIONS

Markets are not created by nature. Their survival does not depend on the sun, the earth, or the original productivity of its soil. Nor does the survival of markets depend on the biology of plants, animals, or people. Markets are made and unmade by human beings who have the option of establishing price-making procedures that are substitutes for markets. There are many different types of political substitutes throughout the world. The critical question is, In view of the performance of these substitutes, have markets become as obsolete as the horse and buggy? Clearly the answer is no.

Markets are an endangered human institution. Economic agents, whether large or small or producers or consumers, prefer not to abide by competition. Each uses political influence to obtain protection from market prices with the belief that a person is entitled to more favorable pricing or a higher wage. Governments tend to accommodate; most governments the world over see markets as a threat to their authority. Where centralized control of the economy is the order of the day, open competitive markets are viewed as a capitalist disease that must be eliminated. In many low-income countries some markets survive, but they are treated as an economic nuisance. High-income, democratic countries are also bent on substituting government prices for market prices. Yet despite all these adversities, markets continue to survive, even if only as last-resort black markets. Although markets have a survival capacity on a par with that of raccoons, they deserve a much better deal than they are receiving. They perform an essential economic function for which there is no substitute. In the United States it is up to the electorate to permit markets to do their thing efficiently.

NOTES

1. Theodore W. Schultz, "Economics and Politics of Agriculture," in T. W. Schultz, ed., *Distortions of Agricultural Incentives* (Bloomington: Indiana University Press, 1978).
2. D. Gale Johnson, "World Agriculture, Commodity Policy and Price Variability," *American Journal of Agricultural Economics* 57(Dec. 1975):823–28.
3. See Theodore W. Schultz, "The Economics of Research and Agricultural Productivity," International Agricultural Development Service Occa-

sional Paper, New York, 1979; T. W. Schultz, "The Politics and Economics of Research," lecture for Museum of Science and Industry Nobel Hall of Science Induction Dinner, Chicago, Ill., April 23, 1980; and T. W. Schultz, "Distortions of Economic Research," speech for Social Science 50th Anniversary Celebration, University of Chicago, December 16, 1979.

4. Cited from Theodore W. Schultz, "Distortions of Information about Food," University of Chicago Agricultural Economics Paper 80:7, for public lecture, Macalester College, Saint Paul, Minn., March 20, 1980.

5. For a useful analysis of this embargo, see Willis Anthony, Willard Cochrane, Martin Christianson, Reynald Dahl, Mary Ryan, and G. Edward Schuh, "The Partial Suspension of Grain Sales to the USSR: An Interim Analysis," Extension Miscellaneous Publication 103, University of Minnesota Agricultural Extension Service, Saint Paul, 1980.

6. Theodore W. Schultz, "On the Economics of Being Poor," *Journal of Political Economy* (Aug. 1980):639–50.

7. Philip Handler, "The Future of American Science," lecture given at Illinois Institute of Technology, Chicago, January 29, 1980.

8. It is hard to believe that the ground beef used in making hamburgers is subject to 41,000 federal-state regulations. See Ted Roselius, "Benefits and Costs of Public Regulation of the Product, Process and Distribution of Ground Beef," unpublished study, Department of Management, Colorado State University, Fort Collins, August 1977.

9. Theodore W. Schultz, ed., *Distortions of Agricultural Incentives* (Bloomington: Indiana University Press, 1978).

10. Philip K. Vergeler, Jr., "Thwarting Energy Independence," *Harper's*, April 1980, pp. 110–13.

11. A. C. Pigou, *The Economics of Welfare* (New York: Macmillan, 1920).

12. Theodore W. Schultz, "Concepts of Entrepreneurship and Agricultural Research" and "Inflationary Expectations and Farmers' Recent Economic Behavior," Don Kaldor Memorial Lecture, Iowa State University, Ames, October 1979 (Staff Paper 102).

6

U.S. Agriculture
and the World Economy

D.   GALE   JOHNSON

THE agriculture of the United States has become a major factor in world trade in terms of both exports and imports. The importance of U.S. agriculture in world trade increased dramatically during the 1970s; the importance of world trade to our agriculture also increased significantly. The prosperity of American agriculture is now very much a function of world demand for agricultural products and how that demand becomes translated into demand for the agricultural products that move in international trade. To a much greater degree than was true in 1970, the prices received by U.S. farmers and their incomes are influenced by decisions made in Brussels, Tokyo, Moscow, Peking, and Warsaw.

The output of one out of every three U.S. acres harvested is exported; three-fifths of our wheat, more than half our soybeans, and almost a third of our corn are consumed outside the United States. We export more agricultural products than we import, and the excess value of exports over imports has averaged approximately $15 billion, increasing to more than $19 billion in 1979–1980.

Significant net agricultural trade surpluses are a recent phenomenon. In other words, the substantial comparative advantage of our agriculture, of which many of us are rightly proud, has reemerged only in recent years. Many may believe such a position has been permanent, but this is not the case.

In terms of a longer historical perspective, the United States

D. Gale Johnson is Eliakim Hastings Moore Distinguished Service Professor and Chairman, Department of Economics, The University of Chicago.

followed the pattern associated with developing countries for the last half of the nineteenth century. As late as 1880 agricultural exports accounted for 80 percent of total exports, and there was a significant excess of agricultural exports over agricultural imports. In the years immediately prior to World War I, agricultural exports still accounted for approximately half of total exports. Even as late as the mid-1920s, when the United States had emerged as a major industrial nation, agricultural exports were 40 percent of total exports.

However, 1922 was the beginning of two decades (except one year) during which the value of U.S. agricultural imports exceeded the value of agricultural exports. Not until the early years of World War II did the United States once again become a net exporter of agricultural products, and this development was almost certainly due to the disruptions of production and transport resulting from the war rather than any fundamental improvement in the comparative advantage of U.S. agriculture.

The net export of agricultural products lasted only a few years. In 1950 imports once again exceeded exports and continued to do so through 1956, even though during most of this period the United States supplied substantial quantities of agricultural products to other nations at low or no cost through its aid programs. It was not until the early 1960s that agricultural exports would have exceeded the agricultural imports if there had been no P.L.-480 program. It is not possible to pinpoint the exact year when the transition would have occurred, since some of the food aid shipments displaced commercial exports.

In fiscal year (FY) 1971 the value of agricultural exports was $8.0 billion with imports at $6.1 billion for a net trade surplus of a little less than $2.0 billion. In FY 1980 the value of agricultural exports was $38 billion with imports at $19 billion for a net trade surplus of $19 billion. The substantial growth in the agricultural trade surplus began in FY 1973 when it reached more than $7 billion.[1]

What was responsible for the large increase in the net agricultural surplus during the 1970s? One of my major objectives is to explain why American agriculture has emerged with such a large export surplus. The significant increase in the U.S. net agricultural trade balance has been the result of maintaining a constant or slightly increasing share of world exports and a declining share of world imports. The reason might be that our barriers to imports increased during the 1970s, but this explanation has little or no validity. The farm products that were heavily protected during the 1960s, such as dairy products and sugar, were the same products heavily protected during the 1970s. Most of our agricultural imports enter either duty-free (rubber, coffee, cocoa, tea, palm oil) or at rates of 5 percent or less. In 1976 the average import duty on dutiable farm products (half the imports) was 7 percent; a decade earlier the duty averaged 10.8 percent.[2]

The only apparent significant increase in the protection of agricultural products in the 1970s compared to the 1960s has been in beef, but this increase has been more apparent than real. We have import restrictions on beef and veal in the guise of voluntary export restraints by the major exporters. The restraints had some effect on beef and veal imports during the 1970s, but it was small. During part of the 1970s the restraints were removed, and in 1974 imports were below the amount that would have been permitted under the program. The maximum restraint in any year has probably been 20 percent of imports or about 2 percent of total beef supply.

The substantial growth in the quantity of exports during the 1970s was due to production increases for major export products and stability in domestic utilization of some of the same products. While total agricultural output increased by 18 percent between 1970 and 1979, livestock output remained unchanged. Thus all the increase in output was in crop output, and nearly all of the increased crop output was available for export. Significant increases in crop output were realized for four major export products—feed grains, food grains, oilseeds, and cotton. The largest production increase was in oilseeds.

During 1978 and 1979 the United States consumed only slightly more grains than during the first two years of the decade. While the domestic use of soybeans has increased gradually during the decade, the percentage of exported soybean production increased from 52 percent for the first two years to 56 percent for the last two years.[3] Restraint in domestic demand for the major export products contributed to the expansion of agricultural exports as well as output growth.

BASIS OF COMPARATIVE ADVANTAGE

The United States stands in a singular trade relationship with the rest of the world. It is a major net exporter of agricultural products and a large net importer of other raw materials. It is a major net exporter of high-technology products such as airplanes, computers, sophisticated military hardware, and complex machinery, but it is a large net importer of a wide variety of standardized manufactured producer and consumer goods. Our major comparative advantages seem to be in two quite disparate areas—high technology products and a primary industry, namely agriculture.

There may well be less of a puzzle in our trade pattern than the previous sentence implies. It can be argued that American agriculture is a high-technology sector of our economy. While there is no clear definition of a high-technology industry or sector, there are certain characteristics that most would agree are associated with such a description: a relatively high ratio of capital to labor, rapid changes in the methods or techniques of production, a high rate of adoption of new and improved inputs, and a relatively large annual flow of resources into research. Where these characteristics prevail, the transfer of technology to other countries is difficult compared to the production of such products as radios, television sets, textiles, or steel. Admittedly the description of a high-technology sector is imprecise and impressionistic, but the indicated characteristics may be helpful in putting the comparative advantage of U.S. agriculture in proper perspective.

Let us look first at two or three inappropriate explanations of the comparative advantage of U.S. agriculture. It is quite common for foreigners, especially those from Western Europe and Japan, to attribute the high productivity of American agriculture to the enormous amount of excellent land and the generally favorable characteristics of our climate. It is true that we are blessed with much land of excellent quality; nowhere else in the world is there an area equivalent to the American Corn Belt. Another explanation for the high productivity is the large size of American farms compared to those that exist in Western Europe and in most other parts of the world outside the centrally planned economies. This statement is empirically valid. A third explanation is that American agriculture employs relatively few workers and the ratio of land area per worker is much greater than almost anywhere else in the world. Comparable ratios exist only in Canada and Australia.

The facts on which the explanations are based can be verified. But the facts, at least in a relative sense, were equally valid when the United States was a net importer of agricultural products. The explanations so frequently offered probably rest upon the mistaken impression that the United States has been a net exporter of agricultural products throughout the past century or more. But agriculture's substantial comparative advantage has emerged quite recently.

The reemergence of U.S. agriculture as a net exporter in the early 1960s was due, in my opinion, to three important factors: modification of our agricultural price and income and exchange rate policies, significant resource adjustments occurring in agriculture after World War II, and the emergence of U.S. agriculture as a high-technology sector. Each was important, and there have been significant interrelationships among the three.

Policy Modifications. During the 1950s, price supports for the major grains and cotton were established at levels significantly above market-clearing prices. Large stocks were accumulated by the government, even though efforts were made to reduce production. Exports declined during the early 1950s; efforts to reduce the accumulation of stocks included the expansion of food aid and the payment of export subsidies on commercial sales. Starting in the late 1950s, price support levels were lowered, and by 1966 supports for most commodities were at or below international prices. When the price supports were above market-clearing levels, subsidies were used to maintain an acceptable level of exports or the quantity was adversely affected. When supports significantly influenced the domestic price, exports were largely determined by the kind and extent of government intervention. When price supports were lowered, the market was permitted to allocate the available supply between domestic and export uses, and there can be little doubt that exports increased significantly as a consequence.

Schuh has argued that overvaluation of the U.S. dollar prior to the 1971 devaluation had imposed substantial costs upon agriculture, including restraining the growth of exports and adding to the resource adjustments required to obtain a satisfactory level of labor returns.[4] The overvaluation of the dollar resulted in lower prices for farm products in the domestic market and greater difficulty in competing for resources with all sectors of the economy except other export-oriented industries. There can be little doubt that the devaluation of the dollar in 1971 and the floating of the dollar in 1973 had the effect of encouraging agricultural exports and improving the relative profitability of agricultural production in the United States. Consequently the change in exchange-rate policy clearly contributed to the size of the net agricultural trade surplus in recent years, even though other factors may have been primarily responsible for the transition from a net import to a net export position.

Resource Adjustments. Significant resource adjustments occurred in agriculture after World War II.[5] These changes included a rapid reduction in the labor input per unit of farm output and an increase in the amount of capital per worker. Agriculture became more fully integrated into the economy and the off-farm income of farm people increased significantly, so that by the mid-1960s approximately half the net income of farm-operator families was derived from off-farm sources. While real farm prices declined by more than 20 percent from the early 1950s to 1970, the per capita disposable income of the farm population increased from about 60 percent of that of the nonfarm population in the early 1950s to about 75 percent by 1970.

High-Technology Sector. A high-technology sector has several characteristics. It requires new knowledge, rapid changes in its capital structure, and a high ratio of capital (both material and human) to labor.

What we describe as modern agriculture is a recent development. The first of the new high-yielding varieties (hybrid corn) became available only during the mid-1930s. It was not planted on half the corn area until 1942. The second important new high-yielding variety (grain sorghums) did not become available until the mid-1950s. Grain yields in the United States in 1930 were very little greater than they had been six decades earlier. The benefits of agricultural research were relatively small and confined primarily to labor-saving inventions until the 1930s. Output-increasing innovations did not occur until there were significant breakthroughs in plant breeding. Once the yield potentials of several major economic crops were increased significantly, numerous other innovations and adjustments occurred that resulted in substantial yield and output increases.

Between 1910–1914 and 1937–1941, crop production per acre increased by 8 percent; between 1937–1941 and 1950–1954, the increase was 16 percent; between 1937–1941 and 1960–1964, the increase was 51 percent; and by 1977–1979, the increase was 120 percent.[6] Almost all the increase in output per acre of cropland occurred after 1955, much of it after 1964.

Farm output per hour of farm work increased even more dramatically over the same period of time—by 960 percent between 1937–1941 and 1977–1979. Output per farm worker doubled between 1937–1941 and 1950–1954, then doubled again by 1960–1964, and more than doubled again by the end of the 1970s.[7]

Modern agriculture is highly dependent upon the services of many other sectors of the economy. It depends upon major continuing research efforts in both the public and private sectors. It depends upon competitive and innovative input sectors that continuously introduce new and improved products and supply them on a timely and assured basis. It depends upon an efficient marketing and transport sector that minimizes the costs of delivering inputs to farms and delivering the output of farms to processors and consumers. American agriculture is favored in all of these areas. This is not to say that similar circumstances do not exist in any other part of the world, but there are only a limited number of countries that provide as effective a setting for agriculture as the United States. Certainly the agricultures of the centrally planned economies are not supported with the same degree of effectiveness nor are the agricultures of the developing countries.

American agriculture is supported by a large and varied set of research institutions. In 1974 approximately a quarter of the world's agricultural research expenditures were made in the United States. One characteristic of agricultural research in the United States is that a much larger percentage of the research is undertaken in the industrial sector than occurs in any other economy. The firms that do research relevant to agriculture are primarily in the agricultural input industries. Such firms obviously draw upon both the basic and applied research of the federal and state agricultural research institutions. A substantial amount of research undertaken in the input-producing firms means a relatively rapid productive utilization of recent research results.

It can also be argued that there is more competition among agricultural research institutions in the United States than in the rest of the world, even within the publicly supported sector. Each state has one or more agricultural experiment stations, and the federal government has a number of different research enterprises. While some of the support for state research comes from the federal government, funds supplied by state governments dominate.

There has been a dramatic increase in the amount of capital per farm worker since 1950. In constant 1978 dollars the value of production assets per farm worker has increased from $40,000 in 1950 to

$150,000 in 1978. If one excludes all land and buildings, the increase has been from approximately $9,000 in 1950 to $28,000 in 1978. A large part of the increase in capital per worker occurred after 1960. In 1978 dollars, production assets per worker in 1960 amounted to $55,000, and in other than land and buildings, $14,000.[8]

In 1976 the 500 largest industrial corporations had $39,000 of assets per employee; production assets per farm worker were almost $125,000 by the end of 1976.[9]

A further indication of the capital intensity of U.S. agriculture is the relative importance of annual capital consumption to net product. In 1977, capital consumption, including the capital consumption allowance, was 40 percent of agriculture's net national product.[10] For all nonfinancial corporations, capital consumption, including the capital consumption allowance, was approximately 12 percent of net domestic product. The high relative capital consumption of agriculture occurs even though its major production asset (namely, land) is not considered in the estimates of capital consumption. Perhaps the most important implication of a high ratio of capital consumption allowances to net product in agriculture is that it indicates a rapid turnover in the stock of capital equipment and the degree to which the capital stock represents the newest and most modern equipment available.

Important as material capital may be in a high-technology sector, human capital is at least as important. One form of human capital is utilized in the development of new knowledge, primarily in public and private research institutions. But material capital and new knowledge must be combined with other resources by the farm operator or entrepreneur.

Modern agriculture is highly complex. Change is rapid; adjustment to new conditions is continuous. There is a continuing flow of new knowledge and new inputs. Agriculture is subject to wider price variations than most other sectors of the economy and in addition is subject to numerous natural conditions over which it has no control. Efficient allocation of resources is both complicated and difficult, requiring a high level of skill. By comparison with other sectors of the economy, farm firms are relatively small. This means that the increasing productivity of agriculture depends upon the capacities of hundreds of thousands of entrepreneurs.

The effects of education on productivity can be divided into two parts, the worker effect and the allocative effect. Following Finis Welch, the worker effect refers to improvement in production as education is increased if other factors of production are held constant. Education may also improve allocative efficiency or ability to acquire and utilize information about costs and the productive characteristics of other inputs, including unfamiliar ones such as new seed varieties, machines, and methods of cultivation. Welch concluded that agriculture is probably atypical inasmuch as a larger share of the productive value of education may refer to allocative ability than in most industries.[11]

Welch's analysis of data for U.S. agriculture shows that the return to the operators with the most education (namely, college graduates) is substantially higher than for all other educational levels. A significant part of the increased return to the college graduate is attributed to expenditures on research that contributes to the changing and dynamic characteristics of agriculture. In effect, as Schultz has argued, "The value of schooling in farming depends on the opportunities that farmers have to modernize their production."[12] As Schultz has noted, modern agriculture is in a continuous state of disequilibrium due to the rapid changes it undergoes as new knowledge and new inputs become available. Before complete adjustment can be made to any set of conditions, new potentialities have been made available. He concludes, "There is enough evidence to give validity to the hypothesis that the ability to deal successfully with economic disequilibria is enhanced by education and that this ability is one of the major benefits of education accruing to people privately in a modernizing economy."[13]

Welch has summarized a number of studies of the returns to education in agriculture related to allocative efficiency. His conclusion was "based on what by now is a large body of accrued evidence, it seems clear that in U.S. agriculture—a particularly dynamic technical setting—education enhances allocative efficiency. Furthermore, increased scale increases incentives for 'correct' decisions and results not only in the 'purchase' of more education for operators of larger farms but in related investments that enhance response."[14]

Since the end of World War II there has been a significant absolute and relative increase in the educational levels of farm operators in the United States. Simultaneously there has been a substantial increase in the scale or size of farms. Since 1960, gross sales per farm, measured in constant dollars, have more than doubled. Another measure of farm scale—farm output per farm—increased 86 percent between 1960 and 1977.[15]

There has been a significant increase in the years of school completed by farmers and farm managers during 1960–1980. For male farmers and farm managers more than twenty-four years old, the median of schooling completed in 1960 was 8.7 years; in 1970 it was 10.6. For all males in the labor force the increase was from 11.0 to 12.3 years. By 1970 the years of school completed had exceeded twelve for three age groups—25–29, 30–34, and 35–44. (In 1960 the median for the 35–44 age group was 9.9.) Available data indicate a continued increase in years of school completed through 1975, especially for the 45–64 age group—from 9.0 years in 1970 to 10.9 years in 1975.

The increase in educational attainment among farm operators is influenced by two factors. The first is that the difference between years of school completed by urban and rural residents has been largely eliminated between 1950 and 1980. The second is occupational mobility. If one follows the age cohorts from 1960 to 1970, the data indicate that among farm operators over 45 in 1970, more years of school were completed than among the same cohort a decade earlier. For the 45–54 age group in 1970, the increase in years of schooling was 0.9 years. For each age group under 45, the percentage of farm operators and managers who had completed at least four years of college doubled between 1960 and 1970. For the cohorts aged 35–44 and 45–54 in 1960, the decline in the number of farm operators was 33 percent and 42 percent, respectively. The decline in the number with four or more years of college was 17 percent and 20 percent. Obviously the farm operators who remained in agriculture had more years of schooling than those who left for other economic activities.[16]

Transferring Agricultural Technology. A characteristic of modern agriculture is that many significant improvements are location-specific. In other words, crop varieties and some production practices are specifically adapted to the soil and climatic conditions of limited geographic areas. In order advantageously to match local conditions with the most appropriate varieties, production methods, and equipment, agriculture must be supplied with the continuing output of sophisticated research and with the required inputs. American agriculture is greatly favored on both counts.

An important implication of location specificity is that it is difficult effectively to transfer varieties and production methods from one part of the world to another. While research has resulted in crop varieties that are less sensitive to certain climatic conditions (such as length of day) than crop varieties developed as recently as 1960, the advantages of technological leadership remain very great.

Maintaining Agriculture's Comparative Advantage. If appropriate
government policies are followed, U.S. agriculture should retain
its comparative advantage into the indefinite future. Continued support of agricultural research is essential. Price and income policies permit the market to allocate available supplies between domestic and
foreign consumers and permit farmers a high degree of freedom in
utilizing their resources efficiently. Agriculture's comparative advantage would be more striking if its major products faced trade barriers in export markets similar to those faced by most industrial
products. We should, of course, reduce the U.S. barriers that interfere
with efficient use of the world's agricultural resources. We have much
to gain from a substantial reduction in trade barriers, including our
own.

IMPLICATIONS OF THE EXPANDED ROLE
OF AGRICULTURAL TRADE

An important economic implication of the enlarged role of
agricultural trade is that farm prices and incomes are influenced quite
directly by the demand for our agricultural exports. There are also important political implications. We are one of the world's largest im-
porters of agricultural products, second only to West Germany in recent years. It is perhaps not totally unexpected that our concern for
what others do to us is greater than our concern for what we do to
others. Consequently, in our trade negotiations and domestic political
policies, more emphasis is given to reducing the variable levies of the
European Community (EC) than to reducing our duties on sugar or
eliminating import quotas on dairy products. There are few organized
domestic groups that support efforts to improve our access to
agricultural imports, but there are numerous well-organized and well-
financed producer groups that work to improve the access afforded to
our agricultural exports.

While a net surplus in agricultural trade only reemerged in the
early 1960s, exports had always been an important component of the
total demand for cotton, wheat, and tobacco. Consequently, from the
beginning of the modern multilateral trade negotiations in the 1930s,
there was a major concern about the reduction of barriers to our
agricultural exports. During the early 1960s it was also recognized that
our ability to export was also a function of our domestic agricultural
and price policies. The political system learned that if prices are set too

high, export sales will suffer. It also learned that government, at least
the U.S. government, was not a very effective instrument for realizing
the full potential of export markets for grains and cotton. The
agricultural policy changes that occurred during the 1960s and early
1970s gradually reduced the role of government in determining the
market prices of farm products. The Food and Agriculture Act of 1977
continued this important trend by transferring most of the price support storage function for the grains to farmers and minimizing and
restricting the role of the Commodity Credit Corporation.

The policy changes were effective in expanding exports and also
generally reducing the importance of government intervention in the
production and marketing of major export crops. But no similar
changes in policy occurred for the farm products for which there is
significant import competition. Thus we find ourselves in a relatively
free-market position regarding the products we export in significant
amounts because we are low-cost producers but with a strong protectionist stand regarding a small number of farm products.

Currently we have strong protective measures for dairy products,
sugar, peanuts, and long-staple cotton. Dairy products and long-
staple cotton are protected by a measure we abhor when imposed by
others, that is, quantitative import quotas. We also impose import
limitations on beef and veal as a result of legislation passed in 1964.
That we engage in the sophistry of negotiating "voluntary restraint"
agreements with the major exporters of beef changes nothing at all.
Nor are we supporters of liberal trade because we suspend import
limitations when domestic prices of beef reach a politically unacceptable level.

Continuing efforts, primarily by producers of fruits and vegetables in Florida, to use marketing orders to restrict importation of
products from Mexico do little for consumers or for reasonable relations with our neighbors to the south. Similarly, efforts to use an-
tidumping legislation to limit imports of Mexican products were
guided by the crassest of protectionist motives. The argument used to
support the claim of dumping was that when supply was large,
perishable farm products were sold at less than cost of production by
Mexican producers. Leaving aside the impossibility of defining cost of
production, such an argument, if supported, would rule out trade in
most farm products at least some of the time. Fortunately, whether for
economic or political reasons, this argument has been rejected by our
government.

These examples show that we do not have a unified policy for trade in agricultural products, although we now have a reasonably consistent policy for almost all the products that we export. We have minimized the role of government in influencing market prices, though we are still not above subsidizing production through the use of target prices and deficiency payments as we do for wheat, barley, and grain sorghums. But we continue to permit special interests to create a fragmented set of trade policies for products for which we are high-cost producers, even when import products are available at lower cost. This is particularly true for sugar and dairy products. Our control over imports of dairy products is justified on the grounds that most dairy products moving in international trade are highly subsidized. There is considerable validity in that argument, but it does not follow that we should maintain dairy price supports at levels that encourage increased output and require rigid import controls. We are a high-cost producer of dairy products. New Zealand and Australia can and do produce at much lower costs than we do, and New Zealand's agriculture is being literally destroyed by trade restrictions imposed by the EC and the United States. The EC also has somewhat lower costs, if you take into account the higher feed costs imposed upon dairy producers by the EC import policy. In other words, in a free-trade situation for both feed and dairy products, EC dairy producers could export significant quantities of manufactured dairy products to the United States. Farm wage rates are not lower in the EC than in the United States, at least when converted at current exchange rates. Thus the competition is not with a low-wage area, an inappropriate argument for protection even when factually correct.

The overvaluation of the dollar, which clearly existed during the 1960s and was not eliminated until 1973, was a factor that inhibited the growth of agricultural exports (and all exports) and encouraged agricultural imports. The continued maintenance of flexible exchange rates is important to effective exploitation of agriculture's export potential.

It is unfortunately true that we do not have a consistent and generally applicable trade policy for all of agriculture. It is slightly ironic that we have been willing to undertake domestic programs and policies to achieve resource adjustments for export products but have generally failed to adopt similar measures for products we import or would import in the absence of protection. We have had no resource adjustment programs for dairy products and beef, nor can one say that we have had effective adjustment programs for sugar, peanuts, or long-staple cotton. Except as an example, long-staple cotton was of little significance; a small number of farmers were heavily protected for years as they produced a rather limited amount. There was never any argument that the producers of long-staple cotton required protection because their incomes were low. Even the impact on international trade was small, since we have provided a limited market. Yet one can regret our national willingness to protect a small number of producers of a relatively unimportant product without regard to the impact, no matter how small, upon the low-income countries that are our competitors.

Our failure to have a consistent trade and domestic policy for agriculture imposes significant costs upon the nation. The costs imposed upon taxpayers and consumers for the protection of dairy products, sugar, and peanuts during 1960–1980 could have paid for the required adjustment programs several times over. Several years ago I estimated that it would be possible to compensate all farmers, farm workers, and sugar processors for the potential losses from abandoning sugar production with four years' worth of the resulting consumer and taxpayer savings.[17] Thus we could have paid for the permanent income benefits from the sugar program several times since 1950, but we have not. We are still engaged in an effort to maintain an uneconomic enterprise in the United States, and our political processes seem incapable of dealing with the problem in terms of the national interest.

A serious secondary consequence of the limitation of grain exports to the Soviet Union has been the increase in the role of government in grain markets. This increase occurred because of the natural political desire to minimize the effects of export limitations upon the incomes (and votes) of grain producers. Several actions were taken, each with the actual or potential effect of increasing the government's role: purchase of four million tons of wheat for increased P.L.-480 shipments and a food security reserve; the increase in the loan, release, and target prices for corn, other feed grains, and wheat; the assumption of contractual obligations involving up to 10 million tons of corn that various firms had contracted to sell to the Soviet Union; and, perhaps most alarming of all, the striking expansion of the program for making alcohol from corn. Alcohol can be made from corn only as a result of massive subsidization. The measures for inducing farmers to put corn in the farmer-held reserve (increasing the reserve storage payment and waiving first-year interest costs for up to 13 million tons entering the reserve) have the potential for increasing the amount of grain owned by the Commodity Credit Corporation in the future. Where local storage limitations made it impossible for farmers to put their corn into the reserve program, direct purchase was made available.

As is often if not always the case, one form of government intervention led to another. Whatever one may think of the international policy merits of the suspension of grain and soybean exports to the Soviet Union, (over and above the 8 million tons of grain permitted under the U.S.–USSR agreement), it must be recognized that important domestic policy implications follow.

NOTES

1. U.S. Department of Agriculture, *Outlook for U.S. Agricultural Exports,* various issues.
2. U.S. Department of Agriculture, Economics, Statistics, and Cooperatives Service, *FATUS,* August 1977, pp. 80–84.
3. Ibid., November 1973, p. 34, and December 1979, p. 34.
4. G. Edward Schuh, "The Exchange Rate and U.S. Agriculture," *American Journal of Agricultural Economics* 56(Feb. 1974):1–13.
5. D. Gale Johnson, "Resource Adjustment in American Agriculture and Agriculture Policy," in William Fellner, ed., *Contemporary Economic Problems 1977* (Washington: American Enterprise Institute 1977), pp. 203–38.
6. U.S. Department of Agriculture, Economic Research Service, *Changes in Farm Production and Efficiency 1977.* Statistical Bulletin 581, November 1977, p. 19, and *Agricultural Outlook,* January-February 1980.
7. *Changes in Farm Production and Efficiency 1977,* p. 45, and *Agricultural Outlook,* 1978, p. 46.
8. Calculated from Board of Governors of the Federal Reserve System, Division of Research and Statistics, *Agricultural Finance Databook: Annual Series,* September 1976, Table 512.1; and U.S. Department of Agriculture, Economics, Statistics, and Cooperatives Service, *Balance Sheet of the Farming Sector, 1978,* Supplement 1, Agricultural Information Bulletin 416, October 1978.
9. U.S. Department of Commerce, Bureau of the Census, *Statistical Abstract of the United States 1977,* p. 563, and *Balance Sheet of the Farming Sector, 1978,* p. 27.
10. *Survey of Current Business,* December 1978, pp. 1–3.
11. Finis Welch, "Education in Production," *Journal of Political Economy* 78(Jan./Feb. 1970):47.
12. Theodore W. Schultz, "The Value of the Ability to Deal with Disequilibria," *Journal of Economic Literature* 13(Sept. 1975):841.
13. Ibid., p. 843.

90   D. GALE JOHNSON

14. Finis Welch, "The Role of Human Investments in Agriculture," in Theodore W. Schultz, ed. *Distortions of Agricultural Incentives* (Bloomington: Indiana University Press, 1978), p. 274.
15. Based on U.S. Department of Agriculture, Economic Research Service, *Changes in Farm Production and Efficiency 1977,* pp. 6–7; *Agricultural Outlook,* December 1978, p. 21; and U.S. Department of Agriculture, *Agricultural Statistics 1977,* p. 422.
16. U.S. Department of Commerce, Bureau of Census, *Census of Population,* 1960 and 1970, Volume 5B, *Educational Attainment*: 1960, Table 8; 1970, Table 11.
17. D. Gale Johnson, *The Sugar Program: Large Costs and Small Benefits* (Washington: American Enterprise Institute, 1974), pp. 81–84.

7

Effect of the Reagan Administration's Macroeconomic Policies and Agricultural Programs on Agriculture

B R U C E   L.   G A R D N E R

THE term "Reaganomics" is usually understood as a reference to the administration's macroeconomic policies, that is, policies in the areas of taxation, monetary growth, the budget, interest rates, and so forth. But an equally if not more important aspect of Reaganomics, as far as agriculture is concerned, is the agricultural programs that will be put in place under the Reagan administration. I shall address both these areas: first, the macroeconomic policies that are the heart of Reaganomics as generally perceived and, second, the administration's agricultural policies. I shall discuss not only traditional commodity programs but also some of the newer regulations of food and agriculture. I shall also make some judgments about how these programs fit into the public interest.

MACROECONOMICS

The macroeconomic side of Reaganomics gets inspiration from two basic propositions. The first is that a smaller government with a smaller budget will be helpful in combating inflation and generally fostering a healthier economy. The second is that lower rates of taxation will lead to more investment by businesses, more work effort by

Bruce L. Gardner is Professor, Department of Agricultural and Resource Economics, University of Maryland, College Park.

individuals, more risk taking by entrepreneurs, and through these means, greater productivity and a higher real income for the economy. These are both theoretical propositions and, as such, subject to dispute. The first goes against the Keynesian idea that a large amount of government expenditure promotes a healthier economy by adding to aggregate demand. The second idea, that lower taxes will increase real income, is consistent with Keynesian theory, but the mechanism is different in Reaganomics—or as it is sometimes called, "supply-side economics."

The characteristic that gives the Reagan administration's macroeconomic approach its uniqueness is the tying of the prescriptions for less government spending and lower taxes to recent theoretical writings somewhat off the main stream of macroeconomic research. The prescriptions themselves are not new; they are standard positions of the Republican party. Moreover, President Jimmy Carter expressed as one of his main goals the reduction of federal spending as a proportion of the Gross National Product (GNP).[1] Presidents John Kennedy and Lyndon Johnson argued for substantial tax cuts and obtained them in 1964—notably, cuts in corporate taxes and rates paid at higher income brackets.[2] The distinguishing feature of the Reagan administration's approach is the theory behind the recommendations. The theory makes a difference in the following way. The mainstream approach has tended to see the economy in terms of a system of equations containing relatively stable parameters, which can be manipulated by altering policy variables (tax rates, the deficit) so as to stabilize the economy. President Reagan, or his advisers, seems not to see the economy this way but rather as a system that cannot be stabilized with the traditional "fine-tuning" tools. The 1982 *Economic Report of the President* states, "This Administration believes that 'fine tuning' of the economy—attempting to offset every fluctuation—is not possible. The information needed to do so is often simply not available, and when it becomes available it is quite likely that underlying conditions will already have changed. As a result, a policy of fine tuning the economy is as likely to be counterproductive as it is to be helpful."[3] Thus the substantial tax and spending changes that have been enacted seem not to have a secure analytical foundation, at least as these policies relate to the 1981–1982 recession, leading some to question whether the administration knows what it is doing.

Not being an expert on macroeconomics, I cannot judge these theoretical issues. It does appear that twenty years ago economists were far too optimistic about their ability to guide and stabilize our economy, but whether current approaches can do better remains to be seen. What I shall consider are the effects these policies will have on U.S. agriculture as they succeed or fail.

We first need to know the aspects of the general economy that are most important in influencing the health of the agricultural economy. I will concentrate on a few basic parameters in the general economy: the rate of inflation, interest rates, and the rate of economic growth.

The effect of inflation on the farm sector is a topic on which one might think that agreement could be readily obtained, but this is far from the case. The consensus at present seems to be that inflation is a bad thing for agriculture, but this view was not always dominant, and in the late nineteenth century many thought it was obvious that the contrary was true. When William Jennings Bryan gave his famous Cross of Gold speech in 1896, the cross on which he saw farmers being crucified was the gold standard. The proposal at that time was to replace the gold standard with free coining of silver, the value of money to be the cheaper of the two metals. The rationale for this switch was apparently that a dual standard would result in a currency that depreciated in value relative to commodities, particularly agricultural, in contrast to gold, which had been appreciating in value. Under the deflationary regime of the late nineteenth century, overall cost-of-living indexes declined by about one third between the mid-1860s and the mid-1890s. At the same time, the prices of farm products fell further, roughly by one half, and there were recurring periods of severe financial distress in U.S. agriculture. Thus, observing that deflation was bad for agriculture, it was inferred by Bryan and the Populists that inflation would be good for agriculture.

This theory appears quite consistent with events in succeeding years. The periods of World War I, World War II, and Korean War inflations were years of prosperity for farmers. The years of the post–World War I recession, which corresponded with a deflationary period, and the Great Depression, which of course saw substantial declines in prices, were bad years for agriculture. They were worse years for agriculture than for the nonfarm sector in terms of per capita income. However, if we look systematically at all the inflationary periods since the first reliable data began to be available around 1910, we do not find it uniformly true that agriculture benefits from inflation or always suffers more than other sectors in deflationary periods.

Since 1910 there have been twenty-four years in which the consumer price index (CPI) rose 4 percent or more: 1910–1920, 1941–1943, 1946–1948, 1951, 1969–1971, and 1973–1981. (Note that the only peacetime inflation was during 1973–1981 and that the period of the Vietnam buildup in 1964–1966 was not inflationary by the 4 percent standard.) Table 7.1 shows what happened to the rate of change of real farm prices (that is, farm prices relative to the CPI) in the inflationary years. On the average, real farm prices rose by 2.35 percent in inflationary years compared to an average decrease of 1.1 percent in the 1910–1980 period as a whole. On the other hand, real land prices increased by 1.3 percent during inflationary years and 0.8 percent in all years, not a statistically significant difference.

It is also interesting to consider what has happened to real aggregate farm income, as estimated by the U.S. Department of Agriculture, during inflationary periods. These data are plotted in Figure 7.1. The circled points and hatched portion of the graph identify the inflationary years. Of the ten highest-income years, eight are in periods of inflation, the other two, 1945–1946, occur in a period of underlying inflation suppressed by wartime controls.

TABLE 7.1.
Rate of Change of Real Farm Prices in Inflationary Years

Year	Percentage change, farm prices[a]
1916	10.7
1917	21.1
1918	− 1.5
1919	− 9.5
1920	−18.6
1941	16.4
1942	13.9
1943	12.0
1946	5.5
1947	2.4
1948	− 4.0
1951	7.5
1969	− 0.5
1970	− 4.0
1971	0.2
1973	8.7
1974	2.1
1975	0.7
1976	− 0.1
1977	− 1.6
1978	0.5
1979	2.1
1980	−10.0
Average	2.35

[a] Percentage change from preceding year average USDA index of prices (deflated by the CPI) received by farmers.

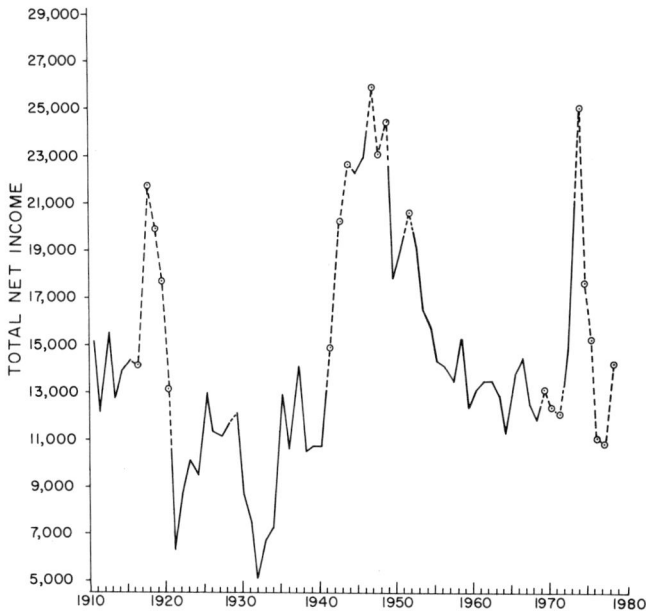

Fig. 7.1. U.S. real net farm income. (Source: U.S. Department of Agriculture, *Farm Income Statistics*, deflated by the Cost-price index.)

These data raise the question of whether the Reagan administration would be doing farmers a favor by halting inflation. Despite the preceding data, I am not ready to opt for more inflation. The main reason is that the farm prosperity associated with historical inflation, when further analyzed, does not seem to be attributable to inflation per se but to other events that have caused both general inflation and higher real farm prices. A full analysis holding other relevant variables constant is not possible to develop here, but I have reported elsewhere results indicating to me that when agricultural supply and export demand are held constant, inflation has significant effect in promoting farm prosperity.[4] On the other hand, it has no significant adverse effect on agriculture either.

The picture becomes more ominous for agriculture if we look at the course of events during the inflationary episodes depicted in Table 7.1 and Figure 7.1. The prosperous periods tend to occur at the beginning of these episodes. As they are prolonged, real farm income and real farm prices tend to fall. This is potentially significant because the most recent inflationary episode is unusual not in its severity (high rate) but in being sustained for so long. It seems evident that in 1980–1981 inflation did not have beneficial results for agriculture. One reason is that expectations in the financial markets caught up in the sense that lenders required unprecedented insurance against decline in the value of the money they are lending. This is the inflation premium in interest rates. These high rates have added a lot to the costs of highly leveraged investors in farming and elsewhere. In these circumstances, the effects of the fight against inflation in the agricultural sector depend on what happens to interest rates.

The primary policy instruments for bringing down the inflation rate pertain to monetary policy. Such is the view expressed by the Reagan administration and by Chairman of the Federal Reserve Board Paul Volcker. Since the Fed is legally independent of the president, it is not obvious that monetary policy under the Reagan administration should be included in Reaganomics, even though the administration has endorsed these policies. Moreover, Volcker was appointed by President Carter. Nonetheless, for the purpose of this discussion, the policy of slowing the rate of growth of monetary aggregates will be included as part of Reaganomics. This approach is better grounded theoretically than the fiscal elements of Reaganomics discussed earlier, has been in place longer, and seems to be having effects of the desired sort. The rate of inflation appeared to be slowing down to a single-digit rate as of 1980. What does this do for agriculture?

It is extraordinarily difficult to say, principally because it is not clear how rapidly interest rates will decline and with what persistence. It does seem clear that interest rates will not remain low (10 percent or less) for a sustained period until inflationary expectations are down to the 6–8 percent level. But in view of the steadily increasing underlying inflation rates during 1966–1981, the establishment of these expectations will be difficult. During those years one would generally have earned profits by betting on acceleration of inflation and lost by betting on deceleration. It will take more than policy plans and promises to offset this experience.

A second difficulty as of early 1982 is that all signs indicate that we remain in a deep recession. Although the farm product markets are no longer as sensitive to business cycles as they were in the 1920s and 1930s, a deep recession adds to the uncertainties facing the farm sector.

Not only is the future course of interest rates uncertain but there is also uncertainty about how interest rates affect agriculture. It is well known that high interest rates cause a cash-flow squeeze for highly in-debted farmers.[5] In the last few years, some agricultural economists have also been pointing to direct links between high interest rates and low commodity prices. There is a long-standing theory that interest rates affect commodity markets by increasing the cost of storage. This means that the spread between cash and expected future prices should rise when interest rates rise. But it is not obvious that the cash price falls (instead of the expected future price rising). Indeed, if only nominal interest rates rise, reflecting anticipated inflation, then the future price should rise and the cash price remain unchanged.

The ideas here remain mostly at the theory or hypothesis stage, although some econometric work has been reported showing that high interest rates have depressed commodity prices in recent years. An in-formal test of the hypothesis shows that as interest rates rose sharply during the summer of 1981, grain prices fell. However, when interest rates peaked and then fell in the autumn of 1982, grain prices fell still lower. So we may reinstate the more standard theory that the decline in grain prices in the summer of 1981 was due to upward revisions in the expected size of U.S. crops. Obviously, more formal testing is in order to resolve this issue.

AGRICULTURAL POLICIES

President Reagan himself seems to have no strong views on agriculture nor any particular interest in or knowledge about it. This puts him in the mainstream of recent presidents (that is, since Jefferson). The consequent tradition of neglect at the highest policy levels has implications for agriculture well worth discussing, but they are not the topic here. In considering policies for the farm and food sector, we should turn to the theme of deregulation. The Reagan administration's ideas about agriculture should be expected to be consistent with a general predilection for less government involvement.

John R. Block, as secretary of agriculture, showed early signs of moving toward deregulation in agriculture. He suggested that the target-price, deficiency-payment schemes, which had been the major form of intervention under the Carter administration, be eliminated. The decision in April 1981 not to raise dairy support prices (however inevitable it may seem on economic grounds in retrospect) was the kind of decision that has often proved impossible to make. While such moves toward disengagement from government involvement have often been suggested by the executive office of the president, particularly by the Office of Management and Budget (OMB) and Council of Economic Advisers, it was a departure to see the Department of Agriculture in the deregulatory ranks.

The Agriculture and Food Act of 1981 was the administration's first major test. Negotiations began on it early in 1981 and continued through autumn. The highlight of the process was the apparent weakness of the administration's drive for a smaller government role in agriculture. The 1981 act turned out to be very similar to the 1977 act that it replaced.

As events have evolved, the Reagan administration's main concern seems to be with the budgetary implications of the new legislation. This evolution is surprising in that it is not quite consistent with the goal of deregulation. This goal, expressed as a market orientation of the farm programs, was pushed further by the Carter administration's target prices coupled with low "loan rates" (market support prices) for cotton and the grains. The next logical step would have been toward less intervention in sugar imports and pricing and the beginnings of less control of marketing and production in peanuts and tobacco. This step may yet emerge, at least for sugar and peanuts, but if so it will not be due to changes proposed by the Reagan administration.

The administration's approach has been to leave these regulatory matters up to Congress, partly as a result of political tradeoffs for what was seen as more fundamental objectives. These concern the macroeconomic elements of Reaganomics discussed earlier—a smaller budget and lower taxes. However, the goal originally stated above was a smaller government, which I would now like to distinguish from the narrower, and I think less meaningful, goal of a smaller budget. There are many activities of a big, active government that add little to budget outlays or may even raise revenues, most notably tariffs; and production controls do not impose upon the treasury as much as upon consumers of the controlled products. In this respect, the administration has gone back from the newer supply-side Reaganomics to the traditional Republicanism of budget balancing, which is favored not only by Republican but by all other OMB directors. David Stockman's revelations in the famous *Atlantic* article simply reveal him as a mainstream occupant of his position.

The Reagan administration has been truer to deregulation in the newer areas of intervention in the food economy. The Federal Grain Inspection Service, as established in the 1977 act, is being cut back.

The Federal Trade Commission has dropped its "shared monopoly" proceedings against the big cereal makers. User fees for inland barge transportation are being considered. Accelerated decontrol of natural gas, crucial to the nitrogenous fertilizer industry, is proposed. Less inspection of meat packing plants is proposed, and there is generally less emphasis on the regulation of food safety and quality. There are moves toward retrenchment in the school lunch and other food aid programs. Potentially important regulatory changes are being discussed in the areas of environmental protection and farmland conservation.

A natural question regarding this deregulatory agenda is what the results will be if it is actually carried out. Whether it will be carried out in the food areas as well as the traditional farm programs will depend ultimately on Congress. This brings in a set of political issues that provide a brake to rapid, large-scale deregulation. The underlying reason is that the business of Congress in practical terms amounts to redistribution of income, and the redistributions enacted by means of regulatory legislation have appeared for good political reasons. Congress produces a supply of legislation according to the demands for redistribution expressed in elections, lobbying, and so forth. These demands will not change quickly. Thus there is a great deal of inertia operating against presidential attempts to make dramatic changes (which is apparently what our founders had in mind). Nonetheless, some changes have been and will be made, and there are implications for agriculture.

I believe that government intervention in the commodity markets as a solution to agriculture's problems over the long term has been a costly delusion. In a book in which I develop this argument, I draw on a long tradition of theoretical and empirical work that leads to the conclusion that the public interest is not well served by intervention in the farm commodity markets.[6] The term "public interest" has different meanings to different people. My definition is that a legitimate government activity (one that violates no one's legal rights) involving gainers and losers is in the public interest if the gains to the gainers exceed the losses to the losers. (Programs that leave everyone better off are in the public interest, but these are omitted from considerations because they do not create problems of political choice and because there are so few of them.) This is the test that the traditional farm programs fail to meet.

This does not imply that all regulation of economic activity is not in the public interest. In Chapter 5, T. W. Schultz distinguishes between activities in which government has a comparative advantage and activities in which markets do. Production and marketing of farm products fall in the latter category. However, it is not possible to make firm judgments in some of the regulatory areas involving the environment and health.

Even in the farm product markets it can be argued that while programs have been costly, the markets have not performed well either. They have been too unstable and have imposed hardships on farmers, as in the Great Depression, with no corresponding gain to consumers in the long run. President Carter's chairman of the Commodity Futures Trading Commission said, "Government is given exactly those tasks which prove too challenging for the invisible hand."[7] However, in the farm commodity markets it is difficult for the government to improve on the market's failures. With respect to the traditional commodity programs, I shall discuss the effects on the farm sector of further deregulation—lower support prices and payments, fewer acreage controls, and less export promotion.

If the market has generated prices that are judged "too low," there are only a few remedies available. All create problems in terms of public interest and the interests of farmers. The government can buy up commodities or pay farmers to store them. The problem for farmers is that if low prices are chronic, the problem is only postponed; but if the problem is only temporary, the stockpiled commodities will hold prices down when the markets strengthen.

The government can also subsidize exports (as has been done to unload stockpiles). This approach provides cheaper food to foreigners than to our own consumers and will not soon be palatable again after the subsidies for Soviet wheat purchases in 1972. It should be recognized that use of public funds for export promotion has essentially the same economic characteristics. Even the relatively interventionist Secretary Robert Bergland had misgivings: "In trade matters, I am under tremendous pressure to continue to expand the sales of grain overseas. My friends, at what price? . . . For every ton of corn we ship abroad we send them two tons of topsoil. Does it make sense? Of course not."[8]

The government can make payments to producers to supplement low farm prices, as we do currently with deficiency payments. But this stimulates even more production. Also, farmers generally do not seem to want to depend on "welfare" checks from the government. Thus Secretary Block opposes this type of program.

Finally, the government can limit production to force prices higher. This has been done not only as an independent step but also in conjunction with price-support and deficiency-payment programs in order to offset their incentives for increased output. While this approach can make farmers better off (at the expense of consumers), it has become increasingly apparent that these programs are not providing nearly the amount of redistribution to farmers that might have been expected. The reason is that production and acreage restrictions impose real costs on farmers, and as the export market becomes larger, the elasticity of demand for U.S. farm products becomes higher. Consequently, it takes substantial production cutbacks and large associated compliance costs paid by farmers to achieve relatively small price gains.

The result is that even though the government may spend $2 billion per year on farm programs, the benefits to producers are substantially smaller. This was not always true but became so as programs initially regarded as emergency or experimental were extended and elaborated year after year.

This implies that deregulation of agriculture may not turn out to be harmful to farmers, despite their political support for farm programs in the past. There is some evidence for this view. Some commodities have never been significantly protected by farm programs for any sustained period, such as soybeans, hogs, and poultry. Some have moved from highly regulated to much smaller programs, notably rice and cotton. The farm sector as a whole is much less affected by commodity programs than was the case twelve to fifteen years ago: the farm-program budget is down substantially in real terms, the support prices are lower, and regulation of production and marketing is less. Although there are difficult analytical problems in estimating the consequences of these deregulatory examples, I do not see evidence that great, or even small economic damage has been done to producers. Therefore, I believe that further experimentation in deregulating agriculture is worth pursuing.

CONCLUSIONS

The unifying feature of the preceding discussion of what Reaganomics will mean for agriculture is uncertainty. There are reasons for optimism about agriculture's future in the absence of government intervention, but there are also substantial risks. The same is true, and probably even more important, for the macroeconomic policies discussed in the first part of this chapter. First, there is the question of whether the monetary policies of 1981 will be maintained, and if they are, what will happen to the rate of inflation. Second, there is the related question of the budget deficit and how it will affect the current recession. Both monetary and fiscal policy will affect interest rates, but how is another uncertainty, compounding the previous two. Finally, even if we knew the future course of inflation, interest rates, and the recession, the implications for agriculture would still be quite uncertain. From my historical search for similar episodes, it seems to me that almost anything could happen.

This is not a time for those averse to risk to be going deeply into debt in large-scale farming. Nonetheless, while current policies in both macroeconomics and agriculture are risky and unproven, it is also true that the preexisting state of affairs had also become precarious. So it might not be a bad time for policymakers to take Mae West's advice: "When you're faced with a choice between two evils, always pick the one you haven't tried before."

NOTES

1. U.S. Council of Economic Advisers, *Economic Reports of the President* (Washington, D.C.: U.S. Govt. Printing Office, 1981), p. 10.
2. Ibid., 1965, p. 65.
3. Economic Report of the President. (Washington, D.C.: U.S. Govt. Printing Office, 1982), p. 36.
4. B. L. Gardner, "On the Power of Macroeconomic Linkages to Explain Events in U.S. Agriculture," *American Journal of Agricultural Economics* 63 (Dec. 1981), pp. 871–77.
5. Luther Tweeten, "Farm Commodity Prices and Income," in *Consensus and Conflict in U.S. Agriculture* (College Station: Texas A & M University Press, 1979).
6. B. L. Gardner, *The Governing of Agriculture* (Lawrence: The Regents Press of Kansas, 1981).
7. James Stone, "Principles of Regulation of Futures Markets," *Journal of Futures Markets* 1(1981):117–21.
8. Remarks by the Secretary of Agriculture before the National Farm Organization, Cincinnati, December 4, 1980, USDA transcript.